EssexWorks.
For a better quality of life

HAD

PRESCHOOL CHOICES

A Parent's Guide

Hilary
Hawkes

Preschool Choices – A Parent's Guide is also available in accessible formats for people with any degree of visual impairment. The large print edition and eBook (with accessibility features enabled) are available from Need2Know. Please let us know if there are any special features you require and we will do our best to accommodate your needs.

First published in Great Britain in 2012 by
Need2Know
Remus House
Coltsfoot Drive
Peterborough
PE2 9BF
Telephone 01733 898103
Fax 01733 313524
www.need2knowbooks.co.uk

Contents

Introduction

If you are the parent or carer of a child aged between two and a half and five, then this book is for you. But if your child is younger then this book will be a useful resource for you too as you look ahead.

The early years in a child's life are a time of great growth and development. Children change and grow physically, emotionally, socially and intellectually at their fastest during their first five years of life. Sometimes it can be hard to keep up with our children's changing needs, behaviours and emerging personalities.

Parents and carers want to help their child become secure and independent. They hope to find and offer them good experiences that will help them reach their potential and develop independence and confidence.

This book will help you:

- Understand the ways in which children develop during their early years.

- Explain some of the things that influence early development.

- Find out where to get initial advice about some common and normal developmental issues that affect a lot of children (such as difficulties with becoming dry at night or during the day, speech problems, shyness, fears, aggression towards other children, etc.).

- Know where to find help and advice if you have concerns.

- Find out what play really is and why it is so important.

- Suggest fun and useful activities that may help your child's all round development.

'Children change and grow physically, emotionally, socially and intellectually at their fastest during their first five years of life.'

Finding a preschool group or activity that is well suited to your child can help him/her develop in many different ways – from acquiring new physical skills to better communication and social skills that can lead to first friendships. If you are looking for groups for parents/carers and children to attend together then there is information on:

- Different types of groups and activities from swimming and gym to baby massage and music.
- Where to find out what is on offer in your area.
- How to decide what will best suit your child.

If you need to find childcare and or preschool education for your child then there are chapters that cover:

- Types of childcare and preschool provision, from childminders and sessional playgroups to all-day day care – private, state and 'voluntary' provision.
- What children learn in nurseries and playgroups.
- How staff take care of your child's education, health and safety.
- What is available to help pay for childcare or where to find out more.

At the back of the book you will find a help list of useful organisations. The website addresses and contact details for each will help you find any further information – try searching for the website title or the subject name if a website address has changed. There is also a book list suggesting further reading and a glossary of some of the terms used in this book.

Chapter One

Early Child Development

During the first four or five years of their lives babies, and young children change, grow and develop at a fast and extraordinary rate.

There are different ways in which children develop and these can be divided into four main areas:

- Physical development.

- Mental or cognitive development.

- Language development.

- Social and emotional development.

While these areas can be thought about separately, they are really inter-related. For example, the young child who has learnt to walk (physical development) can now explore more of his/her environment and discover new things (mental development), will discover new names for new things (language development) and be able to fetch and share toys with carer (social development).

If you have a young child yourself, you will be familiar with the charts and ways of measuring a young child's expected development. Children with special needs may have a different pace of development, of course. However, it's important to remember that all children often reach various milestones at different ages. Some children seem to move through developmental stages more quickly than others. Development charts and stages just show what children are typically able to do at certain ages. It is important to view them as a general guide and not as lists of what children 'ought' to be doing at certain stages or ages.

'Development charts and stages just show what children are typically able to do at certain ages.'

Mental or cognitive development

Mental or cognitive development is about the way someone thinks, reasons, imagines and concentrates. It is also about memory, perceptions and senses. The word 'cognitive' refers to learning or intelligence.

Years ago, people used to think that a person's intelligence was set at birth, but today doctors and scientists involved in neuroscience realise that many influences determine how young children develop cognitively. Most children reach their natural potential as they grow and experience many different things and situations in life. However, if young children are deprived of good relationships and interactions, new experiences and chances to express themselves, then their development in this area may be affected.

Other factors that may affect a child's mental abilities can include whether he or she has a developmental disorder or learning disability. For example, poor physical health and hearing and sight problems will affect how a child learns and understands the world.

'Babies and young children begin to use concepts to think in a more organised way.'

We first learn by linking experiences or consequences with certain sights, sounds, movements etc. Eventually we remember that certain things will happen as the result of other things happening, e.g. if a toddler drops a cup, then he/she learns that the juice spills out; if you sit on your foot for too long it will 'go to sleep' etc.

Some psychologists and researchers call these realisations 'concepts'. Babies and young children begin to use concepts to think in a more organised way, to plan what they will do/play and to understand what might happen next.

In *Childcare and Education*, experts Tina Bruce and Carolyn Meggitt (see the book list) describe how young children go through all sorts of interesting phases as they develop intellectually. They develop different abilities. To begin with they can only concentrate on one thing at a time. Then they begin to understand:

- Sequences – e.g. a piece of round clay can be flattened and then rolled into a sausage shape.
- Differences between similar things – e.g. a black cat and a ginger cat are different types of the same animal.

8

- Similarities between things – e.g. cats, dogs and elephants are all animals but look and behave a bit differently.
- One thing can change into something else (and possibly back again) – e.g. the clay sausage can be flattened again.

Birth to twelve months

To start with, babies just use their senses to explore and make sense of their world. Their sense of touch and movement (sometimes called the 'kinaesthetic sense') enables them to see movement and feel pain. Their sense of taste and smell enables them to find their source of food for example their mother's milk. Their sense of sight enables them to focus on objects (very close to begin with). Hearing means they can respond to their carers' voices or become startled at sudden loud noises.

By five to six months, babies are learning that objects and people continue to exist even when they can't actually still see them. This is called 'object permanence'. They also become a bit more co-ordinated and can, for example, track a moving rattle and reach for and grab it.

By a year old, babies have had enough experiences to have built up some memories. They begin to understand further sequences. For example, they may now be able to anticipate that after a sleep they will have a feed or that if they are put in their pushchair, then they will go outside.

One to two years

By their second birthday most children develop their memories further. They will begin to remember where objects are kept or that they need their shoes to go outside. They become fascinated by all sorts of objects and toys and can occupy themselves with these.

Children this age may also begin to imitate the behaviour of the grown-ups around them, e.g. sweeping a floor, pouring pretend tea, playing with pretend telephones.

They also begin to notice the moods or emotions of other people, if someone is cross or happy, for example.

Two to four years

By the age of four, it is usual for children to have developed what is called 'symbolic' behaviour or play. This means they engage in pretend games and play. They also begin to develop an understanding about how others might be feeling, and this is called 'theory of mind'. It is an essential step in the development of normal empathy.

They also begin to form moral judgements about things and behaviours and can be quite vocal in pointing things out if they appear 'wrong' to them!

They can generally recognise colours, some letters and numbers and can respond correctly to a request to, for example, draw a house or person.

By age four they understand the concepts of past, present and future.

This table shows some examples of cognitive development to four years:

'Between two and four years, most children begin to develop an understanding about how others might be feeling and this is called "theory of mind".'

Age	Able to	Example
Four weeks	Be sensitive to light.	Turns to light.
Eighteen months	Develop symbolic behaviour or play.	Pretend play, such as making cakes with play dough.
Three years	Develop theory of mind.	Understand that Mum/Dad is happy when she/he is smiling and laughing.
Four years	Begin to understand sequences.	Can arrange some simple story pictures in order to show the sequence of a story, e.g. a girl without shoes on, the girl with shoes on and the girl going outside.

Language development

Human beings are natural communicators. We need to communicate with each other in order to be able to live alongside each other.

Babies appear to have a natural urge to communicate their needs and desires and at first this is, of course, without language. Babies use gestures, facial expression, body movements and vocal sounds to express themselves. There are many in-depth and interesting theories and research projects about how babies develop the spoken language of the culture into which they have been born. There are many child development books and online sites that outline these or go into great depth if you are interested to find out more. (See the book list for further information).

Babies gradually progress from hearing and responding to the 'baby' talk that their carers engage in with them (sometimes called 'parentese' language), to recognising that certain sounds (words) have certain meanings. They imitate these sounds and over time acquire more and more meaningful vocal sounds (vocabulary) themselves.

Birth to one year

This stage is sometimes called the pre-linguistic/language stage, but a more accurate description might be to call it an emerging language stage. Sounds babies use to communicate at this age include crying when in need of feeding or comfort, screaming when in discomfort or pain or fearful, sounds of contentment when feeding and cooing in response to carers' voices.

By six months, typical emerging language includes a 'sing-song' type of vocalising to themselves or others and using single or double syllable utterances like dah-dah, ah-ah, er-er etc. Laughing, chuckling and squealing also develop.

By a year old, babies understand very familiar words such as 'mummy', 'daddy', 'cup', 'teddy' etc. and will respond to instructions to 'give cup to Mummy' with encouragement. This indicates that they are beginning to develop their understanding that language carries further meaning – not just names for objects.

One to two years

By the second birthday, babies begin to understand simple instructions such as 'don't touch'. They can also say a few recognisable words themselves. At age two they have about fifty words.

'Babies appear to have a natural urge to communicate their needs and desires.'

Three to four years

During this year there is an explosion in language development as the child talks away to him or herself as he or she plays, copies words heard, listens to other people's talk, asks for names of objects and joins in rhymes and songs.

Four years

At this age children are typically inquisitive and curious and ask constant questions. They also love to chatter and share news and still enjoy talking to themselves or their toys when at play.

By the age of four, a typical child will have a large vocabulary which is clear and intelligible. Speech is usually still occasionally immature e.g. sometimes grammatically incorrect. From about the fourth birthday these inaccuracies generally improve, but some children may still have what are called phonetic substitutions, for example they may say 'wed' instead of 'red'. At this age they also enjoy making up nonsense words.

Some experts believe that because young children have a natural ability to acquire and develop language skills, then this is the best time to learn second languages. Very young children exposed to more than one spoken language at this stage seem to learn both with ease and without too much, if any, confusing of the two.

This table shows some examples of language development to four years:

Age	Able to	Example
Four months	Vocalise pain.	Screaming.
Eighteen months	Learn word for new object.	Points to new object, listens to adult saying the name e.g. 'hat' and then attempts to say word.
Three years	Use personal pronouns and plurals correctly.	Can say, 'There's a car' for one and 'there's cars' for lots and understand the difference.
Four years	Use a large vocabulary.	Describes events or what happened in intelligible way.

Physical development

The first two years of a child's life are the period of most rapid growth. By the end of the first year the body weight has tripled and the child may have grown a further 25 to 30cm in length.

How a child grows is affected by:

- Inherited factors.
- Hormones.
- Nutrition.
- Emotional factors.
- Environmental influences.

Physical development involves gross motor development, which means acquiring large movement skills such as walking, moving whole body, hopping on one foot and fine motor development, for example, being able to pick things up with the fingers, hold and use a pencil etc.

You might notice that your child's development follows a pattern:

- From simple skills developing into more complex ones, e.g. standing with help before standing alone.
- From 'head to toe', e.g. child develops actions that involve use of arms and hands before learning to control legs in crawling or walking.
- Big movements to small, e.g. grasping a bigger object with whole hand before picking up a small object between finger and thumb.
- Responses get smaller or more specific. For example, a small baby will show excitement by wriggling and moving his/her whole body; a four-year-old might just laugh or smile.

Experts Tina Bruce and Carolyn Meggitt describe this pattern in their book *Childcare and Education*. (See the book list.)

Physical development is also about the development of the young child's senses of sight, hearing, smell, touch and taste and another sense known as proprioception:

Sense	Description	Examples of development
Sight	What the child can see.	Most babies are short-sighted until about four months old. Newborns find it hard to follow movement of objects for very long and their eyes lag behind head movement to start with. At six months a baby can turn to look at something moving further away.
Sound	What the child can hear.	At first babies just respond to soothing sounds and alarming sounds. During their first year they learn to recognise their carers' voices and link certain sounds to certain events. E.g. squeakers on toys, sound of juice being poured into cup.
Taste	What the child can taste	From the start, babies like sweet tastes – the mother's milk or formula milk will taste sweet to them.
Smell	What the child can smell	Babies very quickly learn that the smell of milk means a feed.
Touch	What the child can feel physically from external factors	From the start, babies can feel pain, temperature and have a startle reflex called the moro reflex.
Proprioception	Where you are in relation to what is around you.	The baby learns that his/her hand is part of him/her, but the toy he/she is holding is not.

Need2Know

The next chart shows some typical physical development in children from birth to four years:

Age	Typical physical development
Birth to four weeks	Baby lies on front or back with head to one side. If pulled gently to a sitting position the head will lag back. The baby's fists are usually tightly clenched.
Sixteen to twenty weeks	The baby can lift his/her head. Kicks legs vigorously. Beginning to sit with support. When lying on back can put feet in mouth or play with feet.
Six to nine months	The baby can sit without support and may even be able to stand and crawl before the end of nine months. Picks up and moves, shakes, bangs toys and objects with hands.
Eighteen months	The child is walking confidently and can climb onto things. He/she may manage going downstairs by crawling backwards on tummy (not unsupervised though, of course!). The child can build with bricks and grasp a crayon to scribble.
Two years	The child can now run, climb, go up and down steps with two feet on the same step at a time, can walk towards a ball and kick it, can throw overhand, move tricycle with feet on ground, can pick up and manipulate tiny objects between finger and thumb, which is sometimes called the 'pincer' movement or grip.
Three years	Walks up stairs with alternate feet but down with two feet to a step. Can use pedals on tricycle, catch a large ball with extended hands, starts to learn 'dynamic tripod grip' control to use a pencil (i.e. thumb and first two fingers), can build taller brick towers and cut with scissors.
Four years	Sense of balance developing. Can thread beads onto a thread, stand and walk on tiptoe, has good pencil control to draw recognisable objects or letters.

Social and emotional development

Neuroscientists tell us that babies need stable, loving relationships with their carers in order to develop a healthy self-esteem and self-concept. This in turn will enable them to form healthy and confident relationships with others.

Young children need to feel they are loved for who they are. Children who are constantly criticised, put down, emotionally neglected and verbally abused can become aggressive or withdrawn and introverted and may even eventually develop poor mental health conditions. This is because feelings and emotions connected to fear and insecurity that arise from being badly treated or neglected, trigger certain chemical reactions in the brain. This, in turn, effects development of crucial areas of the brain. The way we are treated and made to feel in our very early years literally effects the physical development of an important area of our brains and so determines our future responses and behaviours. A book called *Why Love Matters* by Sheila Gerhadt (Routledge, 2004) is one that gives a full and interesting account of this effect if you would like to find out more. See the book list.

Babies and young children go through stages in their social and emotional development, just as they go through stages in other areas of growth.

'The way we are treated and made to feel in our very early years literally effects the physical development of an important area of our brains and so determines our future responses and behaviours.'

Birth to twelve months

Human beings are relational beings, i.e. we need connections with other people. Babies know this instinctively from birth – they wouldn't survive without the ability to make their needs for survival met. As the bond between baby and carer is established, the baby begins to turn to the carer or their voice when he/she approaches, to react when the carer responds to their cries (e.g. by stopping crying) and they generally seem to find faces interesting to look at.

It is also believed that babies can pick up on how others are feeling. They may become anxious and cry if someone sounds or behaves in an angry or upset manner.

One to two years

Their developing memory and physical skills means they can begin to do more and express themselves with more words and gestures as time goes by. They engage in what is called social referencing, which means looking for approval or help from their carer when trying something new they are not sure about.

Two to three years

This is a time when the child wants to become more independent, which can lead to tantrums and frustration. They like to copy the behaviour of others, to have a go themselves, to get what they want – sometimes successfully and sometimes not!

Children this age can enjoy time away from their main carer (in playgroup sessions, for example), but tend to play alongside others their own age, rather than with or co-operatively.

Three to four years

At this stage children are further developing their 'theory of mind' and this helps them to form friendships and the ability to play with, rather than alongside, other young children. They can begin to grasp the ideas of sharing and taking turns, but need reminding about how to do this.

Three to four-year-olds still need lots of emotional comfort and security though, and can easily become afraid of unfamiliar situations or people.

'Three to four-year-olds still need lots of emotional comfort and security and can easily become afraid of unfamiliar situations or people.'

Four plus

After the fourth birthday young children can appear to be remarkably capable and independent. They have begun to understand social and moral rules and often like to be fiercely law-abiding.

Theories on personality and behaviour

It is important to remember that individual personality and temperament, as well as the amount of encouragement, type of role models and the opportunities children have, all influence how young children behave socially and manage their emotions. Some young children appear to be naturally more sensitive (shy). Others are more confident. Others are more boisterous. Over the last hundred or so years, different theorists who have studied children's backgrounds and behaviours have come up with various ideas as to why this might be. In a very basic and summarised form just some of these theories or ideas include:

'Individual personality and temperament, as well as the amount of encouragement, type of role models and opportunities all influence how young children behave socially and manage their emotions.'

Psychodynamic theories

These theories say that behaviour is the result of our earliest experiences. We go through stages of emotional development and can become stuck at certain levels due to not having our emotional needs met. Attachment to good carers is important and enables babies and young children to progress and adjust to eventually become happily independent.

Behaviourist theories

This theory says that adults 'give' or role model behaviour. Rewards and punishments guide the young child to behaving a certain way.

Socialisation theories

This theory, which evolved from the behaviourist theory, says that the child learns the expected norms of the culture or society in which he/she lives. Primary socialisation is learning to fit in with the family into which the child is born or is growing up. Secondary socialisation is learning to fit in to the wider community.

Social learning theory

Here, children are thought to copy the behaviour of their carers. This copied behaviour may be good or bad.

Socio-biological theory

This theory believes that babies and young children are not entirely influenced by the carers and adults around them. Their own likes and dislikes will affect their behaviour. Children learn for themselves that their own different moods and behaviours get different responses from others. The way people interact with each other affects social development. If a child's own way of behaving is accepted then the child develops a better self-image and so better relationships with others.

See the suggested book list at the end of this book if you are interested in reading more about these theories and others.

Summing Up

- In the first four or five years of life, babies and young children go through enormous changes and many developmental stages. They grow and change physically, learn to speak and communicate.

- Their environment, the experiences they encounter and the quality of care given to them by their main carer(s) help determine their ability to socialise, learn and form good relationships with others.

Chapter Two

Play

What is play?

Play is not just something children do to pass the time. Play is children's purposeful 'work'. It is purposeful because through play children are achieving three main outcomes:

- They are learning about themselves and their abilities.
- They are consolidating things they have learnt and developing physical skills.
- They are learning about others and the world around them through exploring and role playing.

Children's play has certain features. It may be any of the following:

- Thought up by the child him or herself.
- Natural and spontaneous.
- Doesn't particularly have an end target.
- 'Free' – this means it is an activity made up by the child and how and what happens is controlled by the child.
- 'Structured' – this means the child follows an activity or type of game given to him/her by adults.
- Solitary – the child playing alone.
- Sociable – the child involving others in the playing.
- Mainly imaginative or symbolic, such as pretending dolls are having a tea party, or mainly creative/constructive, such as building a model.
- Mainly physical, such as riding a tricycle or climbing a climbing frame.

'Play isn't just something children do to pass the time. Play is children's purposeful "work".'

Sociable play and socio-dramatic play

Up until the age of two to two and a half, young children do not really play socially with other children. Although it is true that babies and toddlers interact and respond to their parents/carers and others, their own initiated play activities are either solitary or parallel (playing alongside rather than with the other child). Experts say there is also another stage in learning to play between two and two and a half when children will occasionally observe or watch others playing but don't join in.

Through sociable play, children experience the behaviours of others. They learn early skills that will help them get along with people in life, such as taking turns, sharing, being fair and considerate. They also learn that other people may have different ideas to their own. They learn about the rules in the culture and society in which they are growing up.

Children who have siblings are likely to learn this 'give and take' and fitting in process earlier than lone children. Parents and carers can help their child's social play development by giving them opportunities to be with other children and by joining in with their children's play themselves.

Social play also helps children develop their language skills as they talk to others, explain what they are doing, ask questions, etc.

Imaginative play and symbolic

Through this type of play children pretend or fantasise. They are often copying events or situations they have observed in real life such as playing 'going to the shops'. Imaginative play can involve dressing up or making or finding props. Imaginative play is often made up as it goes along. For example, in a game of 'playing shops' the child might realise something is needed to represent money and decide that some small pieces of torn up paper can be the money.

Where pretend play involves construction or creativity, the child can develop fine motor skills (e.g. using scissors), eye-hand co-ordination and concentration.

Children can act out or attempt to resolve certain emotional conflicts going on in their lives through imaginative play. Their play can also express moral ideas they have been learning. You might notice this if you overhear your child's conversation with their toys or observe them telling siblings or friends what is and what isn't allowed!

Fantasy play and phantasy play

Role-playing situations which they have not had experience of – such as pretending to fly an aeroplane.

The term 'phantasy play' is used by some researchers to describe children making up games about characters that do not really exist – such as characters from cartoon films.

Physical play

The benefits of physical play are fairly obvious. Through physical movement children learn to develop and refine their muscle control and spatial awareness. There are other benefits, such as learning co-operation when playing with others, self-confidence from gaining new skills – such as how to catch a ball or pedal a tricycle, etc.

Other types of play

Today's children usually have access to different types of technology and computers and television. Used wisely and in moderation, these things can offer children vivid impressions of people and the world around them. Interactive games can reinforce learning, for example, maths or alphabet games on computers.

Experts generally agree that too much exposure to television and computers is bad, partly because it limits the amount of time children engage in more active activities and play. There is also the danger that overexposure may result in too much solitary activity – a kind of 'babysitter' that keeps the child quiet and happy, but distracts them from the kind of stimulating play they really need for their all-round development.

'Children can act out or attempt to resolve certain emotional conflicts going on in their lives through imaginative play.'

Some theories about play

As you can probably imagine, there is no shortage of experts or theorists who have particular views about play. If you are interested in who says what then there are plenty of books on child development and play (see the book list) as well as online sites and resources that go into depth about research findings and conclusions. Different theorists have ideas about what types of play exist (some of which were mentioned previously), as well as what children are actually doing when they play.

The table below shows some theorists whose opinions have influenced the way we treat our children.

Tina Bruce **21st century**	'Free flow' play helps children use experiences to gain new ones. Pretend play is very important and children should be given space and opportunity to be imaginative and spontaneous.
Jerome Bruner **1915**	He thought physical activity was especially important.
Susan Isaacs **1885 to 1948**	This expert thought that play was more important than formal learning until the age of seven. She thought play was especially important as a way for young children to develop and express themselves emotionally.
Lev Vygotsky **1896 to1934**	This theorist thought adults shape children's learning through play by providing them with opportunities to 'learn the next stage'. He called this stretching of the child's ability 'the zone of potential development'. He also thought play was a way children could develop understanding of things they hadn't experienced, e.g. pretending to drive a car.
Jean Piaget **1896 to1980**	Piaget felt that the intellectual stages that children go through from birth meant that they needed to explore and play in different ways at different ages.

Do all children play?

The majority of children will play spontaneously because they all have a desire to explore what they see and hear around them. Children with severe mental disorders may play differently because their ability to absorb and interpret the world around them is impaired. Such children will also react differently to others and so might be unwilling or unable to play with other children/adults.

Researcher in child development, Mary D Sheridan, explains in her book *Play in Early Childhood* (Routledge, London, 2005), that certain situations or circumstances can reduce children's innate desire to explore and play. She says these situations may include illness, abuse and other traumatic events, special needs and poor nutrition.

Most parents notice occasional changes in the way their child normally plays or interacts. This might be seen as a sign of illness, emotional upset or something else. For the majority of children their enthusiasm and interest in play returns once they are better or receive the comfort and reassurance they need with any changes and upsets that might be occurring in their lives.

A permanent inability to play in what most parents view as a 'normal' way can sometimes be one of the first signs that the child has or is developing more complicated problems. For example, a child who is eventually diagnosed with an autism spectrum disorder might show little interest in imaginative games and interacting with other children from an early age.

Children who are deprived (either deliberately or through ignorance) of opportunities to explore and play and interact with others over a long period of time, will develop poor emotional and mental health which might well affect them for the rest of their lives.

'The majority of children will play spontaneously because they all have a desire to explore what they see and hear around them.'

Summing Up

- Play is more than something that children do to keep themselves occupied. Children play in different ways at different times and child development experts have many different theories about styles of play.

- The type of play in which young children engage reflects their stage of development – mentally and emotionally as well as physically. Through play young children discover and learn about themselves, the world and other people. It is therefore important that the adults caring for children provide them with a safe, healthy environment and opportunities for them to explore, imagine, create and interact. The first and most important place for this is at home.

Chapter Three

Learning Through Playing at Home

This chapter looks at some of the ways parents and carers can encourage their child's development and skills through activities and play at home.

Left to their own devices it is true that children will discover and learn and develop through whatever activities or play they might choose. But it is also true that the adults caring for children can influence that learning and development through the way they respond to their children and through what they make available to them.

Developing social and emotional skills

Birth to twelve months

- Most of us parents know the importance of responding to babies when they show signs of distress. Ignoring them at such times and not providing comfort through holding and speaking soothingly is now known to effect the brain development of very young babies. This in turn affects their ability to regulate their own emotions as they get older.

- Make and maintain eye contact when talking to babies. Listen to your baby 'talk' and then respond by talking, singing etc. as this encourages interaction. This helps the baby learn that he/she will get a response to their own 'talking'.

'Make and maintain eye contact when talking to your baby. Listen to your baby "talk" and then respond by talking, singing etc. This encourages interaction.'

- Play with your baby with safe and age-appropriate toys. This will enable them to respond to another person initiating a game, e.g. shaking a rattle, spinning a spinning top for them to watch, demonstrating how to move the moving parts on a cot activity centre etc.

- Provide mobiles that hang over cots or prams. Use bright colours and pictures in furnishings as this gives the baby something interesting to observe and think about.

- Provide safe and age-appropriate reachable toys for the baby to hold and play with. This will encourage him/her to explore and entertain him/herself.

Twelve months to two years

- Make your home toddler-proof so that your child can follow you if you move from room to room. That way you won't need to leave them in a play pen or cot where you won't be able to interact with each other if you are elsewhere.

- Babies and toddlers will often show a natural curiosity when meeting other family members, friends or strangers for the first time. Remember that the way you react to these meetings yourself will influence the way your child will accept new people in the future.

- Very small children can feel secure and good about themselves when they are praised for their efforts. Praise helps build self-esteem and confidence and will influence whether your child will want to try things for themselves in the future. Remember that it is the effort that should be praised – not necessarily the outcome, as this may not always be successful, e.g. the child who attempts to put their shoes on themselves or tidy up their own toys.

Two to five years

- Attempting to do things for themselves and becoming independent is very important to children during this stage of development. Allowing your young child to help you with different tasks is a good way for them to learn how

'Praise helps build self-esteem and confidence and will influence whether your child will want to try things for themselves in the future. Remember that it is the effort that should be praised – not necessarily the outcome, as this may not always be successful.'

good it is to be able to do things themselves. For example, if you need to polish a pair of shoes then let your child (with supervision) polish one shoe while you do the other. Remember to praise their efforts.

- When you can, join in your child's games if they ask you to, or initiate games with your child.

- Find a group and activity for preschool-age children that you think your child might enjoy. These groups are a useful way to introduce young children to mixing with others – they have the added benefit of the parent being there with them, which can help give a sense of security and confidence. Remember to take your child's own unique personality and likes and dislikes into account when choosing activities. The child who is fearful of water probably won't enjoy the toddlers' swimming class very much.

- Put any models your child makes or paintings/drawings they create on display – this will give them a sense of achievement and pride in what they can do. It will also tell your child that their efforts are appreciated and enjoyed by others and that you are interested in what they do.

Developing language and thinking skills

Birth to twelve months

- Providing babies with lots of colourful, safe and interesting things to look at gives them more to watch and think about. Mobiles that move or play music over cots and prams are an example.

- Babies need to be talked to cheerfully and soothingly and they need time to respond in their own 'language'.

- Babies need their carers to talk to them about what they are seeing or hearing or experiencing. This way they hear new words and, in time, connect the words to the object/experience etc.

- Pointing things out in picture book pictures helps babies come across new words and connect words to images.

'Babies need to be talked to cheerfully and soothingly and they need time to respond in their own "language".'

One to two years

▪ Have conversations with your toddler's sounds and words. Respond when they point things out to you and bring toys or objects to you.

▪ Talk about what you are doing together or looking at together.

Two to five years

▪ Look at picture books with your child and talk about the pictures and what is happening. Read your child stories and rhymes. Sing along to music or songs together.

▪ Ask open-ended questions rather than questions that only require a one-word answer such as 'yes' or 'no'. Open-ended questions encourage children to think and put their thoughts into words/sentences.

'Giving children the chance to choose what they want to do encourages thought organising skills and thinking before doing.'

▪ Help your child to correct their speech or grammar by replying in a way that includes giving the correct version. E.g. if a child says, 'It broked' reply with, 'Yes, it broke didn't it?' (Rather than telling the child they've said it wrong!)

▪ Be patient when your child talks to you. Be interested in what they are saying by looking at them and asking questions or responding with encouraging comments.

▪ Encourage your child to problem solve (sometimes called making hypothesis) by asking them what they think will happen if such and such happens or what you should do. Examples might be; you want to go to the park together, how should you get there; it's raining so what should you wear. Very young children can sometimes make incorrect hypothesis and can become obstinate and frustrated if you try to tell them they have got the wrong idea. Sometimes it may be safe to let them discover they are wrong.

▪ Young children develop their abilities to concentrate and remember when given the chance to become absorbed in activities or games that interest them. Giving children the chance to choose what to do encourages thought organising skills and thinking before doing.

Physical development

Birth to twelve months

- Don't leave young babies tucked up and restricted by clothing in cots or prams all the time. When they are awake and content, provide them with a safe and supervised area where they can move freely and reach for their toys – a blanket or activity mat placed on a safe area on the floor is a good idea.

- As your child becomes more mobile make your home baby and toddler-proof so that he/she can crawl and walk around the room to get to his/her toys and explore etc.

One to two years

- Provide a safe outdoor area with age-appropriate toys if you can. Or take your toddler to a safe outdoor area such as a park. From about the age of two, small children can enjoy learning to catch and throw a soft ball, climb small climbing frames and slides, etc.

- Activities and games that encourage development of fine motor control skills and eye-hand co-ordination include puzzles, stacking games, LEGO bricks, pouring water from jugs and other water or sand play, colouring and painting, play dough, dressing dolls, etc.

'Provide a safe outdoor area with age-appropriate toys if you can. Or take your toddler to a safe outdoor area such as a park.'

Two to five years

- At this stage children may be ready to move from using sit-on/ride-on toys to tricycles with pedals. They will often enjoy and be more confident using the play equipment in parks such as slides, climbing frames, etc.

- By the age of five, many children enjoy learning to swim with arm bands etc. – always accompanied and supervised by a competent adult, of course.

- At four or five their fine motor skills also increase, and providing art and craft activities can help with this – e.g. cutting and sticking, threading large beads, tracing, simple board games, etc.

- Young children benefit from being praised for their attempts to dress themselves – gradually learning to manage buckles, zips, buttons where they can.

'Spiritual' development

Even very young children begin to develop a sense of who they are, a sense of pleasure and awe about aspects of the world around them and a sense of what can hurt or comfort another person.

British child psychologist Judy Dunn (see the book list) found that very young children often act out their developing moral sense in games that they play – they show that they are beginning to understand right from wrong and kindness from unkindness.

Parents and carers can help children develop this spiritual and moral aspect of their personalities by trying to act with fairness, showing forgiveness, appreciation of other people, teaching their children to consider the needs of others by considering the needs of others themselves, and by giving children the chance to express their delight and wonder about things they see and experience.

Some common concerns

All children develop at their own pace. Their personal likes and dislikes and their emerging personalities will help determine the kinds of things they show interest in, the ways they cope in different situations and the speed at which they acquire and develop different skills and reach different milestones.

It's normal for parents and carers to become concerned when their child seems slow in achieving a particular ability. Often it turns out that the slowness is not a serious delayed development at all – just the natural pace for that particular child.

Other young children develop habits or fears or other types of behaviour that concern their parents. Some of these might include: failure to become toilet-trained by the expected age (around two or three years of age), failure to become dry at night beyond the age of four or five, being shy or withdrawn in social situations, aggressiveness towards other children, fears of particular things, people or places, nightmares and fussy eating.

Health visitors and GPs are used to giving parents advice about these types of concerns. While the majority of young children will come through these kind of difficulties, it can be reassuring and advisable for parents to discuss any worries they might have with their child's health professional. The following table also offers some tips for dealing with various issues.

Issue	Handy tips
Shyness	Some children are naturally more thoughtful and introspective, and adults need to avoid labelling children as 'shy'. Shyness can be an oversensitivity to outer stimuli. Introverted people need less outer stimuli which can equal less need for socialising with others. Shyness can also be the consequence of too much criticism from parents resulting in loss of confidence. Concentrate on building up your child's self-esteem. Make sure they feel valued for who they are, not just what they can do. Giving a shy child the opportunity to make friends one at a time (rather than in a group) can be helpful. Read *The Highly Sensitive Child* by Elaine Aron. See the book list.
Fears and nightmares	Be understanding and don't belittle your child's fears or tell them not to be silly. With a slightly older preschool child talk to him/her about things you feel scared of yourself and explain what you do to feel less afraid. Allowing your child to stay in close proximity to you, providing distractions, talking about something nice you will do when the fearful situation is over, providing comforters, etc. can all help. Read *Monsters Under the Bed and Other Childhood Fears*. See the book list.

'Be understanding and don't belittle your child's fears or tell them not to be silly.'

Aggression towards other children	It is important for parents or carers to remain calm and in charge of the situation when their child shows anger or aggression. This way the situation is 'contained' and will help the child to feel safe and not so out of control. With a slightly older preschool child try explaining why their behaviour is upsetting or disruptive. Getting down to the child's level and making eye contact will help. See *Toddling to Ten: Your Common Parenting Problems Solved – The Netmums Guide to the Challenges of Childhood* by Netmums and Hollie Smith (Paperback 6 Mar 2008) for some useful insights.
Sibling jealousy	An older child needs to feel as loved and wanted and special as the new addition to the family. Spending time with the jealous child without the other child being present can help. Include your child in some of the decisions you make about a new baby e.g. what colour babygrow you should put the baby in today or which toy would the baby like in the bath, etc. A useful book to read is *Siblings Without Rivalry: How to Help Your Children Live Together So You Can Live Too (How to Help Your Child)* by Adele Faber, Elaine Mazlish and Kimberly Ann Coe (Paperback 1999) .
Toilet-training problems	Don't start too early. The summer months make toilet-training easier. If your child finds this new skill impossible then leave it another few months and then try again. Consider using one of the brands of night-time pants available in shops to help with night-time toilet training. Lift your child out of bed to go to the toilet at least once during the night. Use lots of praise when your child stays dry or gets to the potty/toilet on time. Never scold or punish or ridicule your child if they have accidents or wet the bed. If your child is still not dry at night at the age of five, ask your health visitor or GP for advice. Night-time bed-wetting alarms can work well with some children.

Food fads	Guidelines that can help young children develop healthy eating habits may include: offering babies (who have moved on to solids) and young children a wide variety of foods, encouraging them to feed themselves especially where they show signs of wanting to, arranging food on plates in an interesting and attractive way, avoiding high calorie snacks which may mean children are too full to eat at mealtimes, sitting together and eating as a family if you can – young children copy the habits of adults around them. See the 'fussy eaters' section of the Wiggle into Health site: www.wiggleintohealth.com
Behaviour problems	Children don't misbehave for the sake of misbehaving. Their behaviour is always a reflection of their inner emotional state. Assuming the child does not have any specific special needs, then the following standard behaviour management strategies are recommended by childcare experts: ▪ Set clear and consistent boundaries. ▪ Use positive reward for good behaviour. ▪ Don't tell your child he/she is naughty. It is the behaviour that is unacceptable not your child! ▪ Be a good role model. ▪ With an older preschool child explain in a way your child will understand why certain behaviours are not acceptable. Remember that not all 'toddler tantrums' are bad behaviour and are a developmental stage. See *Terrible Twos: A Parent's Guide* in the book list.
Speech problems	Speak to your child's GP or health visitor if you have concerns about your child's speech. Many children grow out of problems such as stammering or being unable to pronounce certain sounds or letters. A useful book to read is *Does My Child Have a Speech Problem?* by Katherine L Martin. (See the book list).

Summing Up

- Young children learn and develop at a fast rate during the first five years of their lives. How they do this is greatly influenced by the opportunities to play, explore and socialise that they have.

- Parents play a huge part in influencing the emerging skills, abilities and behaviours of their young children.

- Talking to and listening to your baby and young child, playing together, providing age-appropriate toys and games and encouraging contact with other children are all important ways of doing this.

- Look for books and parenting magazines that give ideas about games and activities that are suitable and fun and enhance children's development and skills.

Chapter Four

Activities for Under 5s

Today there are a huge assortment of activities and groups for children of preschool age. Most are intended for parents/carers to attend with their young children. Others provide activities for the children whilst parents/carers remain nearby.

All of these groups claim to have different types of benefits for growth and development. Most of them will help young children get used to social situations and mixing with others. This can be a great benefit when a young child is approaching nursery or school age.

The types of activity groups available varies from area to area and you will need to check information at libraries, family/children's centres or online to see what is available in your area. If you feel your child will enjoy and benefit from a preschool activity group then some of the options are outlined in this chapter.

'Most preschool activity groups will help young children get used to social situations and mixing with others.'

Music and singing

Music and singing groups provide opportunities for young children to experience and enjoy different types of musical instruments, songs and rhymes. Music and singing can play a very beneficial role in the development of young children. While it can have a soothing, cheering and comforting effect on various moods, it also plays a role in speech and language development. It also helps children learn how to express themselves and is a good social interaction exercise.

An example of music classes offered to young children is rhythm time which provides classes for babies, toddlers and preschool age children. The aim of the classes is to help children develop creativity and confidence. See www.rhythmtime.net.

Physical development

These might be classes that involve using apparatus. They are about developing children's physical strength, co-ordination and balance. Parents usually remain to watch or supervise their own child as they move around the apparatus. Some classes end with a class/group time – a chance to develop listening skills, join in together and take turns. The benefits of physical activity classes include: helping your child develop strength and muscle tone, co-ordination and balance skills as well as the social skills of joining in and taking turns and meeting other children. Children who discover that physical activity is enjoyable might go on to want to take up dancing, swimming, football or other active pastimes – with obvious health benefits.

Examples of physical development activity classes are Tumble Tots www. tumbletots.com and MyGym www.my-gym.com.

'Baby massage can help soothe and relax babies who suffer from colic or who are fretful and difficult to calm.'

Baby massage

The aim of baby massage is to sooth and relax babies. It has been known to settle babies who suffer from colic or who are fretful and difficult to calm. See www.busylittleones.co.uk.

Baby signing

The idea behind baby signing is that parents/carers learn to interpret their baby's emotions and needs when they are at a mostly pre-talking stage. Baby signing experts claim that the method can help parents bond with their baby, develop a greater understanding of their needs, help the child develop confidence with communicating and even minimise tantrums. See www.tinytalk.com for more details.

Baby reflexology (foot massage) and yoga

Baby reflexology is a natural 'remedy' that is simple to learn and carry out. It offers parents/carers an additional way of soothing and calming a baby or very young child. Currently, the following websites have useful further information www.busylittleones.co.uk and www.birthlight.com.

Arts and crafts

Most areas of the UK run art and craft classes or groups for under 5s and their parents/carers. Check the online family information services directory for the county in which you live.

There are numerous benefits for children taking part in these classes. Many offer opportunities for children to either have a go at making things themselves, which can give a sense of achievement. Or the classes may also offer group activities so your child can experience joining in and contributing to a group effort, which has obvious social benefits. An example is Doodle and Splat in Scotland: www.doodleandsplat.co.uk.

Cookery

Again, check the online family information services directory for the county in which you live. Benefits are similar to those offered by art and craft classes.

Dance and drama

From the age of about three or four, many children enjoy attending dance classes or taking part in simple acting and story role-playing sessions. These classes can be a fun way to help children develop confidence, co-ordination and fitness. Most areas of the UK will have dance classes aimed at preschool children, so check to see what is available where you live. Many areas of the country also have classes which offer a mixture of dance and drama for children from about age four. Stagecoach and Sonnet Theatre Stage School classes for children from four years upwards are examples. Check online or at a local library to see what is available locally for you.

Speech and language development

These aim to be fun classes that help preschool children develop communication skills. Parents/carers attend the sessions with their child and children are divided into age groups so that activities are age/stage appropriate. An example is Talking Tots. See www.talkingtots.info. The classes aim to help children develop concentration, attention span, social and pre-literacy skills.

Library storytimes

'Talking tots provides fun classes that help preschool children develop communication skills.'

Locate your local/nearest library and enquire about storytimes for under 5s. Some libraries offer these free events on a weekly, fortnightly or monthly basis. Libraries also sometimes invite authors to hold sessions for children – so look out for writers of picture book stories etc. whose sessions may entertain and benefit your child. Listening to stories helps children's pre-literacy skills, and develops listening, thinking, concentrating and understanding. It also increases children's knowledge of the world and can help children develop an interest in reading themselves later on, with obvious educational and personal benefits.

Some bookshops also hold story events for young children. They may be occasional or regular and are often advertised in the shop in advance.

Family centre activities

Children's/family centres are located in most towns and areas of cities and provide a huge variety of activities for preschool-age children. These activities might include: stay and play sessions, art and craft, story and rhyme times, physical play and music sessions. Many of these activities are free or low cost.

Family centres also provide information and support for parents of babies and young children. They are also a good place to go to enquire about other preschool activities on offer in your area.

Swimming for under 5s

Parent/carer with child swimming sessions are offered by many leisure centres/ swimming pools. Lessons for children to attend without the parent/carer being in the water with them usually start for children over four years of age. The emphasis of these sessions/lessons is on having fun in the water and acquiring confidence.

Parent and toddler groups

Parents/carers attend these groups with their toddler-age children. They are generally set up by groups of local parents who run the groups voluntarily. The groups offer small children a chance to play with a selection of toys (indoor and outdoor activities) and mix with other children. At the same time they are a good way for parents/carers of young children to meet other parents/carers.

Toy libraries

There are still toy libraries in many areas of the UK. They offer free or low cost loan of carefully selected games and toys and sometimes play sessions too. See National Association of Toy and Leisure Libraries www.natll.org.uk. Some exist especially for children who have special needs.

Online activities

Online sites for young children may offer stories, crafts, educational games etc.

The following table shows some sources for finding online activities, resources and games that are suitable for preschool children to do with a parent or carer at home. Your child will gain the most from these if you sit with him/her and play the games together for short periods of time.

'Children's/ family centres are located in most towns and areas of cities and provide a huge variety of activities for preschool- age children.'

Resource	Description	Benefits
Fisher Price Online games and activities See www.fisher-price.com	Games and activities for toddlers and preschool-age children.	Helps children to learn shapes, colours, numbers, sequences, letters, phonics, visual discrimination etc.
Little Tiger Press Online Awesome Activities. See www.littletigerpress.com.	Games and activities for young children.	Helps develop thinking, discriminatory and language skills.
Little Chestnuts Stories, rhymes and games that encourage pre-literacy and communication skills. www.hilaryhawkes.co.uk/littlechestnuts.	Online and down-loadable stories, rhymes and language games for three to six-year-olds. Parent and child together activities.	Helps teach alphabet recognition. Promotes listening, thinking and communication skills through stories, rhymes and games.
Sesame Street Online games and activities with the characters from the popular TV series. See www.littletigerpress.com/lyndall/activity/.htm	Games and activities for preschool-age children.	A variety of interactive and fun games that help preschool-age children develop number, letter, shape, colour knowledge.

Summing Up

- If you decide your child will benefit from joining a preschool activity or group, then look in your area for classes that you think will be most enjoyable and beneficial for him/her. Remember to ask other parents for their views of the classes and ask the activity group organisers if you and your child can have a trial session first before you commit to a whole course or term of classes.

- If you have to work full-time it may be difficult to find time and energy to take your child to an activity group. Many childminders include taking their small groups of toddlers and preschool children to under-5 activities in the care they offer. Or you may be able to attend with your child on an occasional/ during holidays/weekends basis. Helping children to have fun alongside other children of the same age can help them develop confidence and experience new environments and activities.

'Remember to ask other parents for their views of the classes and ask the activity group organisers if you and your child can have a trial session first before you commit to a whole course or term of classes.'

Chapter Five

Types of Education and Care

Most parents look for some type of childcare or preschool education for their child at some point. Parents who work full-time or longer part-time days will need settings that provide care that cover the hours they work. These parents often choose day care nurseries that are open from early morning to late afternoon all year round. Other parents may prefer to use childminders who might take their child to preschool or nursery sessions as part of the service they offer. (Here, the word 'setting' refers to preschools, nurseries, nursery classes and all other groups for under 5s).

Parents working part-time or who do not work are more likely to choose sessional preschools or nursery schools which offer two to three hour sessions or 'school day' (nine am to three pm) sessions.

This chapter explains some of the different types of care and preschool provision available in the UK.

Regional differences

Provision for under 5s and entry into school classes varies depending where in the UK you live. So check with your Local Education Authority for details about school starting ages and how children can enter school before age five.

England	English under 5 providers follow the Early Years Foundation Stage. Children can start full-time formal schooling at four years old, but compulsory education begins the term after the fifth birthday.	For more information see www.directgov.uk
Northern Ireland	A child who is four years old on or before 1 July in any year starts primary school on 1 September that year.	See www.nidirect.gov.uk and follow the links for information about education
Scotland	The 'Scottish Curriculum for Excellence' has a three to five section which covers its curriculum requirements and aims for under 5s.	See the Learning and Teaching Scotland website: www.ltscotland.org.uk/earlyyears/curriculum/parentsandcarers.asp
Wales	Children can start full-time formal schooling at the beginning of the term in which they become five. Compulsory education begins the term after the fifth birthday	For more information see www.directgov.uk

'Day nurseries offer all day care for children under five years of age. Many make provision for very young babies.'

The terminology used to state which class or stage children are at can be confusing. Some areas use the word 'preschool' for children from around age two, 'nursery class' from around age three to four, 'Reception class' at age four to five and then 'Year 1' at or by age five. Some children, depending on where their birthday falls, may miss out on the reception class and go from nursery to Year 1.

In other areas the name 'Foundation Stage 3', 'Foundation Stage 2', 'Foundation Stage 1' and then 'Year 1' are used for these four stages instead. The words 'Foundation Stage' are abbreviated to 'FS' – i.e. FS1, FS2, FS3.

Even within the same area some schools may admit children at earlier ages into their first classes than others. Some have just one intake of school starters (in September) and others admit pupils at the start of other terms too.

So it is necessary to check what system or options exist in your own area. Remember also, that there is a difference between the age at which children *may* begin formal schooling and the age at which compulsory education begins. Most children now begin at an earlier age than compulsory school age. Parents sometimes feel they must take up the offer of a place early in order to secure a place at the primary school.

Day nurseries

Day nurseries offer all day care for children under five years of age. Many make provision for very young babies. They are staffed by a mix of qualified and pre-qualified staff. A supervisor or manager or nursery nurse is usually someone who has what is known as a level three qualification at the very least, plus experience. Level three is a qualification in childcare and/education at approximately A level standard. Many supervisors and managers have achieved much higher qualifications – level four or degree level or actual childcare/teaching degrees, post graduate qualifications or early years professional status. Staff who have undertaken higher level training, specialising in the care and education of young children are often called early years practitioners.

Sometimes children in day nurseries are organised into age groups and generally kept separate so that they can be given age-appropriate care and activities. In other day nurseries children are placed in groups of mixed ages.

Staff:child ratio should be high:

- Children under 2 years 1:3.
- Children aged 2-3 years 1:4.
- Children aged 3 years plus 1:8 – or more (1:13) if a qualified teacher is present
- Children in Reception classes (or FS1) 1:30 with a qualified teacher and a nursery or teaching assistant

As young children attending day care centres are there for such a long time, the day is arranged so that they have opportunities for free play, educational activities, sleep and rest, meals and breaks etc. They follow the Early Years Foundation Stage (EYFS – see the next chapter), or UK regional equivalent.

Nursery schools

Nursery schools generally offer shorter days and may be term-time only. They generally cater for children aged two plus.

Nursery schools follow the Early Years Foundation Stage.

Some nursery schools also follow a particular philosophy or approach to childcare and education. For example:

'Some nursery schools also follow a particular philosophy or approach to childcare and education.'

- Montessori – Maria Montessori (1870 to 1952) was a doctor working in Italy in the early nineteen hundreds. She devised an educational programme for a group of children who had learning disabilities and quickly realised her methods could be used to teach all children. The Montessori curriculum divides the classroom into five areas which offer activities for the children to use by themselves (after being shown how). The apparatus are 'mistake proof' to a large extent, which means the child can see if they have done the activity correctly. The five areas are everyday practical life (dressing, pouring, opening lids etc.), language, maths, sensorial (activities that encourage use of senses) and cultural (geography). See www.montessori.org.uk. Ideally staff are qualified Montessori teachers. A Montessori teacher has a level four or degree level equivalent qualification in early years.

- Rudolf Steiner – Known as Waldorf Schools. Rudolf Steiner (1861 to 1925) was an Austrian academic who used the ideas of a philosopher called Friedrich Froebel to set up a school for children of workers at the Waldorf Astoria cigarette factory in 1911. His emphasis was on a non-academic and unhurried curriculum. Steiner schools today admit pupils at age three. Children who remain with the school throughout their school years have the same teacher until they leave. See www.steinerwaldorf.org. Teachers at these schools are specially trained in the Steiner method of teaching and hold specialist qualifications.

Friedrich Froebel, who was such an influence to Steiner, set up the first kindergarten for young children in Germany in 1837.

- Faith schools/nurseries. Sometimes churches and religious groups set up their own preschool groups to cater for the children of their own members – many also offer places to any children in the local community. Their purpose is to care for and educate young children in ways that are in keeping with their own particular faith or beliefs.

Private nursery schools charge termly fees which can range from £700 to over £2,000 per term.

Case study

'I chose a day nursery for my eighteen month old son, Nathan. I was going back to work four days a week and needed somewhere that offered long days of care right through the year.

'The day care centre is open from eight in the morning so I drop Nathan off on my way to work. I pick him up on my way home around half past four to five o'clock.

'Nathan settled in really easily straight away. There weren't any problems. They provide a room for the little ones to have a rest after lunch so he gets his daytime nap.

'The nursery has a cook and the children's lunch and tea is prepared on the premises. Nathan doesn't seem to have had any complaints about the food.

'He loves his key person who is always there to meet us when we arrive and she hands him back to me at home time. She's always got some comments about what he's been up to which is nice.

'I think Nathan is quite a laid-back and extrovert child and the nursery suits him. He seems to like being around other people and having lots of things to do and activities.'

Laura, mum to Nathan.

Preschool playgroups

Playgroups offer term-time sessional care for children aged two to starting school age. The sessions are generally morning or afternoon only. Some offer an additional lunchtime hour which can lengthen the session. Staff often have the preschool qualification called Diploma in Preschool Practice, which is a level three qualification.

Playgroups also follow the Early Years Foundation Stage (EYFS) and, perhaps more than any other type of under 5s setting, encourage parents to get involved by helping in sessions and being on the preschool committee. Playgroups sometimes have their own building in the grounds of a primary school or a room in a family centre. Sometimes they hire community halls to hold their sessions.

Playgroup session costs can vary from £4 to £7 per session.

'Playgroups offer term-time sessional care for children aged two to starting school age.'

Nursery classes in schools

Nursery classes attached to primary schools admit children a certain number of terms before they become statutory school age. The age at which children can be admitted varies depending on where in the UK you live. There may be up to thirty children in a class. The person in charge of the class will be a qualified early years teacher, i.e. one who holds a teaching degree/post graduate qualification. Because of the larger number of children in the class, there will be a teaching or nursery assistant too.

The children often wear a uniform like the rest of the school children. Their days may be mornings or afternoons only or all day and are term time only.

Many schools now have Foundation Stage units where children are admitted into a nursery class after their third birthday and then, in time, progress to Year 1 by the age of five.

Childminders

These days, childminders have to have completed a recognisable training course. Many do additional training which enables them to offer children the Early Years Foundation Stage curriculum. Like nurseries and preschools, they keep written observational records of the children in their care and must follow strict adult/child ratios and safety adaptations to their homes.

Childminders probably offer parents the most flexible childcare arrangements and some will also allow children to stay overnight when needed. They must be registered to provide this additional facility. Some childminders will take the children in their care to activity groups, playgroups etc. if parents want this. For more details about childminders see the National Childminding Association at www.ncma.org.uk.

Childminders charge anything from £2.50 to £7.50 per child per hour. They usually offer parents discounts for siblings. No more than three under 5s can be looked after by one childminder and of this number no more than one child can be under the age of twelve months.

School 'wrap-around' care

Many primary schools have breakfast sessions or clubs and afterschool clubs. This kind of 'wrap-around' care means that working parents can leave their children at school earlier in the morning and collect them later in the afternoon, when they have finished their own working day. Children have breakfast and a light tea and supervised activities are provided. The sessions are normally staffed by qualified play staff rather than teachers. There is a charge for the sessions.

Crèches

Crèches provide temporary or occasional childcare for children. They may be permanent settings in, for example, leisure centres or shopping malls. Or they may be on site temporarily, at a conference or special event for example.

'Schools often have Foundation Stage Units where children are admitted into a nursery class after their third birthday and then, in time, progress to the Reception class before entering Year One by the age of five.'

Crèches have to follow legislation about staffing suitability and safety of children, but do not have to be registered with Ofsted (Office for Standards in Education, Childrens' Services and Skills) if the children stay for less than two hours a day or if parents remain on the premises.

For details about crèches in your area contact your local Family Information Service. You can find their contact details on the Directgov website – www. directgov.uk.

Case study

'The most important consideration for us when we looked for childcare for Bethany (age two) was flexibility. Mark and I are both self-employed and so our working hours can be different each week or every day.

'We decided on a childminder because she is able to be as flexible as we need. If we need to leave Bethany at half seven up to lunchtime then we can. Equally, she'll care for Bethany all day if we need that too. We pay for the hours she actually has Bethany and not for sessions like in day nurseries.

'In a few months time Bethany will be old enough to go to the local preschool which is where I want her to go. Most of the children from there go on to the local primary school and it's nice if they already have friends when they do that. Our childminder is local so she'll take Bethany to the preschool sessions and collect her for us. Then she'll hold on to her until I can be there to pick her up after lunch.

'Bethany is good friends with a little boy who goes to her childminder too. She gets on well with other children there as well. It's a home environment which is what I like for her.'

Caitlin and Mark, parents to Bethany

Free places for three and four-year-olds

In England, Scotland and Wales, all children aged three and four are entitled to a free early education place.

In England, the free sessions are for 15 hours a week. Parents can spread this flexibly over three or more days a week during term time.

In Wales, the free sessions are for at least ten hours a week. There is no minimum to the number of weeks in a year the sessions should be provided.

Not all nurseries, schools, playgroups or childminders take part in the scheme to provide free early education places. Each local education authority holds lists of nurseries/preschools which provide these free early education sessions. Most settings do provide them, but not all. Nursery classes that are attached to schools and approved childminders can also provide the free sessions. The scheme is also used by private schools and private nurseries. This means that even if the school or group would normally charge fees, you don't pay for the entitled free hours.

A lot of parents want their child to attend longer hours and more days than the free places allow for and so pay for the additional hours and sessions. For more details about the scheme see: www.childcarelink.gov.uk, or phone 0800 234 6346. Use the same website to check for up-to-date information if and when the scheme extends to two-year-olds.

For parents in Scotland, the preschool education page at www.scottishchildcare.gov.uk is also useful.

The free places scheme operates in Northern Ireland too, but tends to vary from area to area. Individual schools and preschool groups in the scheme provide information about how to apply for a place and about the education they offer.

Some employers offer parents help with paying for childcare costs. For current information see 'Paying for childcare – getting help from your employer' which is currently downloadable from the www.directgov.uk website at the parents section of the website. This section of their website also includes information on child tax credits and flexible working arrangements.

Parents who need additional help in meeting the cost of preschool education should see the 'getting help with preschool costs' section of the Directgov website. Use the links to find the help that applies to your situation.

'Once you have decided what type of preschool, nursery or childcare would suit your child, you will need to contact the setting to make an appointment to visit.'

Choosing your child's preschool or nursery

Once you have decided what type of preschool, nursery or childcare would suit your child, you will need to contact the setting to make an appointment to visit.

You might find it helpful to ask other parents who already have, or have had, children at the setting you are considering what they think of it. Check out the setting's website and ask for a prospectus too, if they have one. Ask for information about the Early Years Foundation Stage curriculum.

When you visit, it can be helpful to take someone with you – your partner, a friend etc. A second person can help with remembering all the questions you might want to ask and can take care of your child while you concentrate on talking to the supervisor/teacher etc.

Questions to ask

It should go without saying that all staff should have been CRB (Criminal Records Bureau) checked and vetted. The setting should also be Oftsed registered and receiving inspection visits and reports. Whether you are considering a childminder, a day nursery or a sessional preschool you will need to find out the following:

- Are staff suitably qualified?

- What are staff ratios?

- Does the setting looking 'safe' from a common sense point of view e.g. secure playgrounds and gates, stair gates in use, items and toys within children's reach are age appropriate. Are door alarms and access keys/ codes used?

- If babies and toddlers are catered for as well as three and four-year-olds are they looked after in separate areas or mixed age groups?

- Is at least one member of staff a qualified first aider?

- Ask to see their Ofsted inspection report and written policies on behaviour and the curriculum they offer.

- Is there a quieter area for rest and sleep if children stay all day or for very long sessions?

- Do they use a 'key person' system where a small number of children are allocated one particular member of staff who pays particular attention to those children's needs and development?

54

- What routines are set out for the day/sessions?

- How do they observe and keep records of the children and how often do they hold progress report meetings with parents?

- If you wanted to speak to a member of staff regularly about how your child was doing, when would you be able to do that?

- If your child has special dietary requirements how will they cater for that?

- If your child needs medication – either temporarily or permanently – how will they deal with that?

- If your child has specific special needs can they tailor activities to suit him/her? See chapter 7 for more information about young children with special needs in preschools.

- Do children get taken on outings and how are these supervised?

Once you have decided which nursery/care setting is right for your child then you will need to ensure that:

- Registration details about you and your child include your emergency contact details.

- You can meet the costs of the sessions if fees are charged.

- You understand the terms of giving notice if you wish to withdraw your child at any point.

- Your child will be offered taster sessions and introductory sessions if possible.

'It is sensible for you to stay with your child on the first visit.'

Introductory sessions

The purpose of introductory sessions is to help your child get used to attending the nursery/preschool/being left with the childminder.

It is sensible for you to stay with your child on the first visit. Staff will encourage your child to try activities that interest him/her. Some children are more adventurous than others in new environments, while others will prefer to just sit quietly with mum or dad at first.

Some settings like the parent/carer to attend with the child a few times before leaving him/her for part of the session and then eventually leaving him/her for the entire session. You and your child's key person/teacher will be able to judge when your child is ready to be left. Many children do become upset when left the first few times, but skilled and experienced staff are usually able to help the child settle after a short time.

Settling in problems

Occasionally, settling in does take longer. You can help your child settle by allowing him/her to take a favourite toy/comfort item or story book that staff can read to your child or leave an item that belongs to you – maybe your scarf, gloves. However, some nurseries have reasons for not allowing this – so check first! If possible, don't expose your child to too many sessions at once – let him/her get used to attending before increasing days/hours. Make sure you always return on time to collect your child.

'You can help your child settle by allowing him/her to take a favourite toy/comfort item.'

Many parents do worry about leaving an upset and clingy child with a childminder or nursery. It can be distressing to know you have to rush away to get to work. Remember though, that what your child is experiencing is perfectly natural – being separated from his/her main caregiver is hard-wired into young children as something they must interpret as not good! However, with practice they soon learn that spending some time away from their mum/dad is alright after all. At some stage we all learnt this. Remember too, that staff are qualified and experienced in caring for young children and will contact you if there are any real concerns.

If, after a few months, your child still appears to be reluctant to go to the nursery and unhappy whilst there, then it may be a good idea to look at other types of childcare/nurseries. Sometimes children fit better into some environments than others – a smaller nursery or childminder's home environment may suit some children better than a large day care centre, for example.

56

Complaints

Preschool and nursery settings should have a procedure in place for dealing with parents' concerns and complaints, should they arise.

Most concerns that parents have are sorted easily when the parent speaks to the staff. If you have a concern or complaint about the care or education your child is receiving in preschool/childcare, then first of all speak to the person who deals most with your child –i.e. his/her key person/teacher. Most concerns and worries can be resolved when talked over. If you are still unhappy after this then speak to the nursery manager or supervisor.

Your child's childminder/nursery/teacher should have the interests and care of all the children as their first priority and will want to understand and resolve any upsets and worries that parents bring to them.

Childcare standards are regulated by the Office for Standards in Education, Children's Services and Skills (Ofsted), so if your concerns are of a more serious nature then you could contact them for advice. See the help list.

'Preschool and nursery settings should have a procedure in place for dealing with parents' concerns and complaints, should they arise.'

Summing Up

- In most areas of the UK there is a wide choice of childcare and nursery provision for children under the age of five.

- Asking other parents for their recommendations and visiting local schools/ childminders etc. will help you get the best idea of what would suit your child and meet the childcare needs you have.

- The funding available for three and four-year-olds now means that most children will experience some time in preschool before they reach statutory school age.

- A lot of working parents change the type of childcare their child receives as the child gets older. For example, starting with a childminder and then moving on to nursery school as they approach school age.

- Your own needs as a working parent, your own budget, what is available locally and your child's personality will all influence the choices you make.

Need2Know

Chapter Six

What Children Learn in Preschool

Early years providers (except for toddler groups, nannies and short-term care facilities like crèches) follow a structure or curriculum of learning, development and care for children from birth to five years old. This is called the Early Years Foundation Stage of care and education (EYFS) and it aims to enable children to learn through a range of activities and experiences.

By April 2012, a revised EYFS framework will be issued by the government, following a review by Dame Clare Tickell. Many teachers and other professionals involved in teaching and caring for young children felt the older EYFS version (from 2008) was too bureaucratic and not focused enough on children's learning.

Their concerns included the following points:

- The curriculum was too prescriptive for use with babies, toddlers and very young children.

- It prevented some schools/groups from fully employing their own particular philosophies or beliefs.

- It was very difficult for very small settings and some childminders to cope with the regulations and administrative matters.

- There were too many 'goals' and desirable outcomes.

- Assessments on children required a lot of administration time that took staff away from the job of caring for the children.

- It meant settings could lose their individuality and so parents then had less real choice when it came to selecting childcare/nurseries.

The revised curriculum claims to take account of a lot of the earlier concerns about the original EYFS and to build on and improve the original framework.

Nurseries and schools have to show (via their Ofsted inspections and reports) that they are offering children activities and learning experiences that promote the goals of the EYFS.

The curriculum or 'practice' covers six areas of development and learning and these are:

- Personal, Social and Emotional Development (and spiritual).
- Communication, Language and Literacy (or Communication and Language).
- Mathematical Development (or Problem Solving, Reasoning and Numeracy).
- Physical Development.
- Knowledge and Understanding of the World.
- Creative Development, (or Expressive Art and Design).

This means that young children are not being merely supervised while they play, but are being offered activities that have been thought out and designed to contribute to their all-round development.

For example, staff speak to children in a way that encourages conversation and develops their thinking and verbal skills. Group activities and circle times help children learn listening, sharing and turn-taking skills. Games, activities and themed projects teach children early pre-literacy, numerical skills and about the world and people around them.

Planning

Teachers/nursery staff 'plan' the sessions for the term/half term/year. Some settings will use 'long-term' plans which will show how they will implement the goals of the EYFS over a whole school year, term or half term. They also have short-term plans which may be a more detailed plan of what will happen over the next week that fits in with the long-term plans. Staff will think about and note down which areas of learning each activity will promote. A week's plan for the theme 'people who help us: the post office' could look like this:

'Nurseries and schools have to show (via their Ofsted inspections and reports) that they are offering children activities and learning experiences that promote the goals of the EYFS.'

Time	PSED	CLL or CL	Maths/PSRN	KUW	Physical/PD	Creative/CD Or EAD
9.30	Choosing from a variety of activities.	Talking together during activities.	Weighing pretend parcels.	Talking together about how letters and parcels get to their destinations.		Make post vans from junk modelling materials.
10.30	Morning break and outdoor play – taking turns, considering others, helping, sharing.	Listening to instructions.		Talk about weather outside, look at nursery garden together, make road in chalk for pretend post vans.	Using playground apparatus, tricycles etc.	Talking about colours outside e.g. flowers etc.
11.15	Greeting visitor.	Listening to visitor (postman), asking questions, taking turns.		Finding out about the jobs that postmen/women do.	Aware of space needed for self and others when playing outdoors.	
11.45 To home time	Considering others when listening to story.	Sitting quietly, concentrating.	Counting the postman's letters in the story.	Recognising the work of the postman in the story.		

The key to the abbreviations:
- PSED – Personal, Social and Emotional Development.
- CLL – Communication, Language and Literacy (or CL=Communication and Language).
- KUW – Knowledge and Understanding of the World.
- PSRN – Problem Solving, Reasoning and Numeracy (or M=Mathematics).
- PD – Physical Development.
- CD – Creative Development (or EAD=Expressive Art and Design).

Other settings do not make such pre-decided plans. They follow a more open system of providing activities and play materials that enhance children's all round development. Their assessments and observations of every child help them to see how individual children are progressing in every area.

Most good preschool providers also know the importance of allowing children plenty of time to develop their play and activities rather than having short time slots for doing particular parts of the timetable. Free-flow play is regarded as important: children are also allowed to move from indoor activities to outdoor play activities as they wish for part of the session if not for all of the session.

Important considerations for staff

'Within the class or group will be a mix of abilities and personalities. The special needs of children who have specific learning difficulties or other needs will be taken into account.'

When nursery staff plan or provide activities for the children, they take certain important considerations into account. In *Planning Play and the Early Years* (see the book list), experts Penny Tassoni's and Karen Hucker's 'keys to good practice' include:

- Safety.
- The needs of individual children.
- The importance of being non-discriminatory.
- The skills and abilities of staff.
- The involvement of parents.
- The need to leave room for adjusting and replanning if necessary.
- Readiness for school.

Safety

Staff must ensure that children are safe within the nursery environment. Safety includes: physically safe, because activities and apparatus meet required safety standards and are well maintained; safe because locks and alarms are used on outer doors, gates to playgrounds, etc.; safe because staff are vetted and safe because all children are treated with care and respect.

The needs of individual children

Within the class or group will be a mix of abilities and personalities. The special needs of children who have specific learning difficulties or other needs will be taken into account. Some of these children will have their own Individual Education Plan and the support of a special support member of staff. (See chapter 7 for information on children with special needs in preschool).

Staff will also take the ages of the children into account when planning, and may provide different levels of the same activity so that some children can undertake a more challenging task if they are able to.

Being non-discriminatory

Practitioners must ensure that no child in their setting is excluded or discriminated against because of their background, disabilities, gender, etc. This means that staff must ensure that all children can take part and feel they are equally catered for.

The skills and abilities of staff

Some staff may have many years of valuable experience and others may be newly qualified or even volunteer students on work experience placements. Staff will ensure that the people with the right level of experience and expertise will supervise or lead certain activities.

Involvement of parents

Most settings welcome parent volunteers who can help give children some extra attention or free up time for staff by undertaking some of the routine chores in the nursery. Parents are also encouraged to support their child's learning and experience by bringing in items that support themes and talking to their children about what they do in nursery.

Parents are also informed about assessments made on their children. Information about the Early Years Foundation Stage and what happens in preschool should be available for them. Ideally, there should be a partnership feel between the preschool and the family. This is especially helpful where a child may have difficulties.

Leaving room for adjustments

There should be a certain amount of flexibility when it comes to any planned activities. A particular outing might not be possible if the weather is bad, for example, or someone might forget the ingredients for the biscuits the children were going to bake! So having reserve activities may be useful.

Readiness for school

An important aim of the preschool is to help children become ready for school. What happens in preschool needs to help children develop certain skills that they will need for this important step. The prime areas might be regarded as their personal, social and emotional development, their communication and language skills and their physical maturity. Preschool education aims to cater for children's all-round progress and development.

Your child's progress: observations

Nursery settings use a key person (or equivalent) scheme. This is where each teacher/member of staff is allocated a small number of children in which to take a particular interest. Each key person will have about the same number of children – though new or less experienced staff may have less. In some schools/nurseries a key person will have four to six children. In larger classes they may have to have quite a few more.

The key person will make individual observations of each of their children. They may spend one or two sessions a term observing and making notes about an individual child. The purpose of these observations is to see if the child is making expected progress and to determine if there are any particular areas where a child may not be moving forward.

'Most settings welcome parent volunteers who can help give children some extra attention or free up time for staff by undertaking some of the routine chores in the nursery.'

A key person may spend time making additional observations if any particular concerns about a child have been raised.

The purpose of these observations is:

- To inform staff and parents of the children's progress.
- To find out if there are any areas of concern.
- To see if that child's particular needs are being met.
- To influence future activity plans.

If a child has special needs then the observations may be shared with any other professionals involved in that child's care.

Observations and assessments of an individual child should never be shared outside of the school without the consent of that particular child's parents.

Your child's progress: Individual Learning Plans

Each child in the setting will have an Individual Learning Plan. In the term prior to a child starting school, staff complete a detailed record of progress or profile of assessment that will be passed on to the school. This gives the school some useful information about each child.

Your child's key person will help your child reach the next stage/goal by setting manageable aims or goals. For example, a four-year-old who holds pencils in such a way that prevents them from drawing/forming letters etc. might have the following strategy written into their Individual Learning Plan:

'Each teacher/ member of staff is allocated a small number of children in which to take a particular interest.'

- Staff to demonstrate correct grip prior to handing him/her a pencil.
- Use rubber grips on pencils to aid child's use of them.
- Staff to provide games/activities that promote the correct grip (i.e. holding an item between the thumb and first two fingers).

Most settings will offer parent-teacher meetings. These give parents a chance to discuss their child's progress at preschool/nursery. Many settings will also provide older preschool children's parents with written reports – perhaps at the end of an academic year.

Summing Up

- Registered nurseries and childcare settings follow a curriculum that adheres to the six areas of development and learning. These are Personal, Social and Emotional Development, Communication, Language and Literacy, Mathematics (or Problem Solving, Reasoning and Numeracy), Knowledge and Understanding of the World, Physical and Creative Development. The qualifications and curriculum authority framework for this curriculum is known as the Early Years Foundation Stage.

- Staff in preschools and nurseries provide age and stage-appropriate activities that help promote growth and learning in these six areas of development.

- They observe and keep records of children's progress.

- Today, while the emphasis in childcare settings is on learning through play, there is also a more formal focus which is brought about through the choosing/planning and assessing of activities and recording of progress.

Chapter Seven

Preschool and Special Needs

If you are the parent of a young child who has special needs, then the job of finding suitable childcare or nursery provision may need extra careful thought. You will want to ensure that those who care for your child in your absence have a good understanding of your child's condition or needs and are able to provide the right sort of environment, care, support and learning experiences for him/her.

Some children's needs may be too great for them to be integrated into mainstream nursery or day care settings. For example, for a child with severe autism who cannot cope with the noise and unpredictable behaviour of other children and who finds this very stressful, a mainstream setting may not be the best option for such a child.

Other children whose special needs may be anything from milder autism, dyspraxia, sight and hearing disorders, ADHD or some physical disabilities may be quite well catered for in mainstream settings. Talk to your child's healthcare professionals and determine together what is best for your individual child. Find out if you qualify for additional financial assistance to meet the cost of childcare.

'Some children's needs may be too great for them to be integrated into mainstream nursery or day care settings.'

What are special needs?

Physical disabilities	The child has significant impairment of mobility or co-ordination which is either permanent or temporary.
Neurological/developmental disorder	Example autism, dyspraxia.
Speech or language disorders	Examples: stammering, delayed speech.
Specific learning disability	Such as difficulties experienced by children with Down's syndrome.
Medical condition	Examples are asthma, epilepsy, cystic fibrosis, severe allergies.
Sight and hearing disorders	Examples are partial or complete loss of vision. Partial or complete loss of hearing.
Terminal illnesses	Examples are childhood cancers.
Emotional problems	Examples are fears, phobias, extreme shyness.
Conditions that cause 'behavioural' problems	Examples are hyperactivity attention deficit disorder.
Giftedness	Being significantly advanced in terms of cognitive/mental/artistic ability.

The table above shows some of the categories of special needs that young children may have. While some children may have very obvious needs (e.g. a child with a physical disability who uses a wheelchair), others may have less obvious and often almost invisible conditions, such as milder autism or epilepsy.

Need2Know

Mainstream settings and care

The Disability and Equality Act 2010 states that it is illegal for schools and education providers to discriminate against anyone on the basis of a disability. (see www.directgov.co.uk accessed November 2011).

With regards to very young children, the Special Educational Needs Code of Practice, to which preschool settings must adhere, sets out ways in which children with special needs can be supported and included in nurseries/ playgroups etc., as far as possible.

Your local council, Sure Start Children's Centre or Family Centre, if you have one, should be able to give advice to parents looking for childcare or education for under 5s. An organisation called Contact a Family (www.cafamily. org.uk) has a lot of useful information.

A scheme called Early Years Action is used by preschool providers to give support and special assistance to children with special needs. Staff will assess your child and may write, or at least verbally agree, an Individual Education Plan (IEP) with short-term goals. They may also provide a special assistant or one-to-one helper for your child – depending on the severity of the child's needs. An Individual Behaviour Plan (IBP) may also be devised for a child with behavioural problems.

Some children may need more support than that, which is provided by the Early Years Action. They may need Early Years Action Plus. This is where outside professional helpers may be involved in helping your child – for example, if speech therapy is needed. If a specialist, like a speech therapist, assesses the child then their suggestions can be included in the IEP.

Information or assessments about a child should not be shared with other professionals or anyone else without their parents' knowledge or consent.

Where a lot of extra support for a child is required, local authorities might want to make a statutory assessment known as a Statement of Educational Needs. It is rare for a very young child to be statemented, but if you and your child's nursery feel this is needed in order for the child to be supported correctly, then you can apply to your Local Education Authority for this to happen.

'A scheme called Early Years Action is used by preschool providers to give support and special assistance to children with special needs.'

Currently, more information about young children and special needs can be found at: www.direct.gov.uk/en/Parents/Preschooldevelopmentandlearning/SpecialEducationalNeeds

Before you visit a nursery setting or childminder, find out how they support children with special needs. Questions you will need to ask when you visit with your child may include:

- Do they understand your child's condition/special needs?
- Have they taught/looked after children with similar difficulties in the past?
- How large are classes/how many children attend each session?
- What is the staff:child ratio?
- Can your child have a one-to-one helper?
- Can your child have extra 'settling in' sessions if required?
- If appropriate, how will staff handle your child's medication?
- Show the teacher your Family File if you are on the Family Support Programme. This will make your child's disorder and any help/treatment/support already being received clearer.

'Before you visit a nursery setting or childminder find out how they support children with special needs.'

Special schools

You may know that mainstream settings will be unable to cater for your child. You and your child's health-care professional may decide that a preschool that specialises in caring for children with more complex special needs is the best option.

Your Local Education Authority will have information about what kind of provision is available in your area. Check for information and advice available for families of special needs children from your local Family Information Service.

You may decide to find a private special nursery/preschool or school. Check information provided by charities that support children with your child's condition. For example, if your young child has autism then the National Autistic Society's website and magazine has information about specialist preschool provision. www.autism.org.uk

The advantages of getting your child into a special school may include:

- You and your child's needs may be better understood.
- Staff are trained to care for special needs children.
- Possible transport to and from the school for children.
- Buildings better adapted for wheelchair users – doorways, toilets, etc.
- Special equipment or sensory areas/rooms that benefit certain children.
- The chance to meet other parents in the same position as you.

Further special needs provision

In addition to childcare and nursery education for your child, you may also want to find out if there are any groups or activities in your area especially for children with particular special needs. Your local Family Information Services should be able to give you advice and details. Depending on where you are, groups and activities can include:

- Special play days/toy libraries.
- Music groups.
- Parent and child toddler groups.
- Sensory play buses or play sessions elsewhere.
- Riding for the disabled.

'In addition to childcare and nursery education for your child, you may also want to find out if there are any groups or activities in your area especially for children with particular special needs.'

Case study – Chloe

Chloe is four years old. She has cystic fibrosis and needs frequent visits to hospital and physiotherapy. Her parents have to go through a physiotherapy routine with her every day which involves exercises that prevent the build-up of mucus in her lungs.

Chloe needs daily medication and a special diet. She becomes very tired very easily and has a poor immune system which means she is susceptible to catching any viruses or illnesses that might be going round.

Chloe's parents want her to attend the local primary school which has a nursery class attached.

Staff at the nursery class have to administer Chloe's medication mid-morning each day during term time. One member of staff is appointed to do this. The medication is kept in a locked cupboard in the classroom.

Because of Chloe's special diet requirements she brings in to nursery her own snack. Chloe's mum also leaves an extra small healthy snack at nursery, in case Chloe's energy levels drop before the end of the long morning session.

Chloe joins in with all the activities provided for the children and her key person pays her special attention during outdoor or physical play.

Case Study – Leah

Leah, aged four, has general delayed development and learning difficulties. She is still being assessed to see if she has a particular diagnosable disorder.

Leah's parents felt that the local mainstream nurseries and playgroups would be unsuitable for her – due to the size of classes. So they enquired about enrolling their daughter in a special preschool for children with a variety of special needs.

Leah attends two morning sessions a week. The children are not expected to arrive by a particular start time, but any time during the first hour of the session. This makes life easier for Leah's parents who often find she is reluctant to get dressed. Morning routines seem to be particularly stressful for Leah, so being able to go at her own pace with regards to getting ready and getting to preschool is much better.

A speech and language therapist visits the preschool each week and Leah is one of the children who has sessions with her. Leah enjoys the calming effect of the sensory room and she normally makes straight for his area of the school on arrival.

Summing Up

- There is more to consider when looking for childcare for a child with special needs. Many children do manage well in mainstream settings where they are given extra support. Other children, some who may have more complex difficulties, are better catered for in special schools or settings that specialise in caring for children with particular or various disorders.

- Finding the right place for your child means that he/she will experience time away from you, learn to mix with other children and experience a variety of activities and learning experiences. It will also give you some all-important respite from caring for your child.

- A good source for further reading is Sarah Newman's *Small Steps Forward* (Jessica Kingsley Publishers, 1999) which includes information for parents of children with different special needs on where to get support, advice and information, your child's development, finding support for yourself and your family, activities that encourage growth and development, and the assessment process.

Chapter Eight

Becoming School Age

Starting full-time school is a big step for all children and their families. The age at which a full-time school place is offered varies slightly depending on where in the UK you live. However, by just before or just after the fifth birthday most children have made the transition from being a preschooler to attending full-time school.

Parents generally receive a letter from their Local Education Authority informing them of the school entry procedure and how to get their child into the state school of their choice. If you want your child to attend a private school, then you need to contact the school early (sometimes several years early) so that your child's name can be placed on the list for entry into the required year. Many independent primary schools (often called pre-preparatory schools) require prospective pupils to take an entrance 'test'. You will need to contact individual schools to find out what this involves.

This chapter is about preparing your child and yourself for the transition to full-time school. For types of schooling and entry procedures, contact your Local Education Authority and local primary school. You might like to obtain another book in this series called *Primary School Education: A Parent's Guide* for more information.

'Starting full-time school is a big step for all children and their families.'

Getting ready at preschool

Hopefully, gone are the years when some young children go straight from being at home with a parent or carer to being suddenly deposited at school all day without any kind of preparation at all.

Today, the majority of children will have spent some time outside of their own home away from their main carers. This may have been by attending a preschool, day nursery or in the care of a childminder with other children. It is fairly obvious that these types of settings will have helped your child get used to the idea of being elsewhere and with other children. So in what ways do early years practitioners help to prepare your child for school?

Being away from the main carer

Getting used to being away from the main carer (usually mum or dad) helps young children prepare for the big step of going to 'big' school later on. For many parents who have to work, this is an inevitable arrangement that has to be made. Children who have settled with a childminder, in a preschool, or nursery class, generally find the move to formal schooling less stressful.

Of course, a school environment is different to a nursery environment. It is much larger for a start and your child will come across children who are much older. Classrooms may be bigger, there are more staff in the buildings and routines may be more formal. School break times/playtimes in larger playgrounds, PE and lunchtimes in halls will be whole new experiences for most very young children.

'Getting used to being away from their main carer helps young children prepare for the big step of going to "big" school later on.'

Lunchtimes

Many, if not most, nursery and preschool settings, now offer lunchtime sessions and all day sessions. If your child is attending these then they go some way to preparing him/her for having to stay all day at school later on. Children will be used to taking their own lunch boxes and sitting together to eat under supervision. Staff usually sit with the children and encourage them to eat enough. They will also encourage washing hands, tidying up and being considerate towards others sitting at the table too. Staff will give extra attention to any children who may, at first, be unhappy with the idea of staying for lunch or all day at nursery.

You can help your child by allowing them to choose or take along their favourite lunch box. While you will want the food they take to be healthy, experiment with preparing it in fun and attractive ways. For example, cutting into interesting shapes, placing food in small different coloured containers, etc. Your child might even like to help you prepare the lunch. You could sometimes include an extra surprise treat. Remember, don't put in food you know your child won't eat!

Playtimes

A lot of schools now provide a separate outside play area for the youngest children and these areas tend to resemble preschool outside play areas. Staff often put out play equipment and there may be a sand pit area and climbing apparatus. The differences your child will find at school, though, may include more children in the play area, longer playtimes, not being allowed indoors to play instead, not being allowed indoors without asking permission and being supervised by different staff to those in the classroom. PE lessons in school halls will probably be a new experience too – along with having to change into different clothing for this lesson.

Even so, outdoor play areas at nursery schools can help your child prepare for mixing with larger groups of children, sharing play equipment, learning to put on their own shoes/boots/coats, etc. – all of which they will need to manage with less teacher supervision once in 'big' school.

Children who are more used to suggesting games or being included with others and 'joining in' may enjoy school playtimes more. Staff in preschools often include adult-initiated games during outdoor playtime and encourage all children to take part. Playing an organised game where everyone joins in can sometimes be more helpful to, for example, very shy children who might otherwise find themselves alone.

Routines

The routine of attending preschool sessions or nursery will help young children prepare for starting school.

Most preschools begin each session at a set time. Children will have a particular peg in the cloakroom for their coats, bags, etc. and maybe somewhere in particular to put lunch boxes or anything they may have brought from home. Foundation Stage classes in school will be the same.

Sitting together in a group at registration time will be another event that occurs in both settings. Circle times and smaller group times help children get used to listening and concentrating, alongside others. Staff in preschools will encourage children to contribute ideas or answers during circle or group times.

The layout of the preschool classroom often mimics the layout of the school classroom. Children can move from one activity to another and there will be small group activities where a member of staff will supervise. The environment may not be so different then. When young children become more comfortable in one environment, then they are often more likely to adjust to a new but similar environment.

Getting used to following the instructions of staff as they look after the children in preschool also prepares children for school. 'Keeping the rules' and knowing what behaviours are acceptable and what behaviours are not acceptable is all part of the experience of attending preschool nurseries.

Social skills

Young children who attend preschool will learn a lot about getting along with other children. They will be used to being part of a group or class and they will learn that other people often have other ideas and likes and dislikes compared to their own. They will also discover what happens when others disagree with you or won't share and how teachers/grown-ups deal with this.

Some young children are lucky enough to move on to school with one or two friends from nursery or preschool. Many parents see this as one of the advantages of enrolling children in their local nursery and primary. Having familiar friends around can boost confidence and make the first days of school more enjoyable.

Learning through play

When children begin 'big' school they find some aspects that are not so different to preschool. The classrooms for Foundation Stage children will have a lot of free-play areas. Activities such as sand play, dress up, construction toys, book corners, etc. are available as part of the curriculum. The timetable includes times for this free-flow play, when children can choose an activity from the indoor as well as an outdoor area that is close to the classroom.

More formal learning

More formal learning and teaching takes place in school settings, but children can get used to small amounts of this in preschool. Many nurseries plan activities for one-to-one or small group work for pre-literacy or pre-maths teaching, for example.

Many of the 'stepping stones' that work towards the goals of the early years curriculum can be achieved whilst children are in preschool or nursery schools. For example, in preschool years children often:

- Learn to link sounds to letters – learning to recognise the alphabet.
- Are able to say the alphabet.
- Learn to write their names and simple words.
- Learn to recognise simple words in the environment around them.
- Recognise numbers up to nine and count ten everyday objects.
- Understand the concepts of more or less/adding and subtracting.
- Understand quantities and see sequences and patterns.
- Understand words that describe position such as 'inside', 'behind', etc.
- Recognise shapes.

(From *Curriculum Guidance for the Foundation Stage, QCDA, 2000*.)

'More formal learning and teaching takes place in school settings, but children can get used to small amounts of this in preschool.'

School visits and visit days

Some preschools are 'feeder' schools for their local primaries and as such are able to take groups of children into the primary school to visit the class they would join on starting school. These 'taster' mornings/days can be very useful in offering prospective pupils some introductory experiences of what it will be like at that school.

Some primary schools invite nursery children to special events, such as sports days or end of term plays etc. This is also another useful experience and chance to see classrooms, the assembly hall and meet teachers, etc.

In a similar way, some nurseries and preschools are able to invite the Foundation class teachers to visit children at the nursery.

Getting ready at home

It isn't just the job of nursery classes and preschools to prepare young children for the big step of starting school. There is a lot parents and families can do to make this major event in every child's life go more smoothly.

All children and all families are different, but some good aims to have include:

- Helping your child to feel confident about themselves.
- Encouraging your child's friendships.
- Sending your child to school visit days where they are offered.
- Attending meetings for prospective parents.
- Making sure your child can use the toilet independently and can manage things such as using a knife and fork, a normal cup, changing their clothes (managing buttons, zips, shoes, etc.).
- Not showing you are anxious yourself (if you are).
- Not having unrealistic expectations about your child.
- Allowing your child to settle in at their own pace.

Helping your child to feel confident

This can often be about letting your child know you value them for who they are not just for the things they can do – even at this very young age. Young children can learn to be shy and lack confidence around other people and in new situations when they have had too much criticism or over-correction by parents. Showing that you are interested in and understand your child's likes and dislikes and personality characteristics will help them develop a feeling of self-worth. This in turn will help them feel more secure in new situations.

Encouraging friendships

Encourage the early friendships that your child forms at nursery or preschool or other groups he/she might attend. Having a friend round to play now and then and being invited to play with other children in their homes helps children develop deeper friendships. It also helps children learn how to share their possessions, discover that other people often have different ways of doing things, different types of homes, etc. All this helps your child learn about getting along with other people. Your own friendships and the way you treat others will be an influence on how your child develops their own relationships too.

Visit days and meetings for parents

Your child's prospective school should let you know in good time of any approaching visit days for its new intake of pupils. Keep the days clear of other activities so that your child can attend. Put the date on a calendar for your child to see and 'talk up' the event so that your child sees it as something exciting to look forward to. If your child has a friend or two who will be going to the same visit day then think about meeting up and arriving at school together.

Meetings for prospective parents are a chance for you to look around the school if you haven't already done so, meet other parents, meet the teachers, find out more information about the school, the curriculum, the timetable and ask any questions you might have.

Independence

Teachers of very young children are aware that their pupils may still need help or supervision with getting changed, going to the toilet, etc. If your child can manage going to the toilet, hand washing, dressing themselves as independently as possible, then they will obviously find doing these things in school much easier. So make it a goal for your child to be able to manage as independently as possible by the time they begin school. But don't be anxious if you think this might be a problem for your child. Foundation Stage teachers understand that some children take longer to become independent and most children this age still have occasional accidents or need some help with zips, buttons, shoes, etc.

'If your child can manage going to the toilet, hand washing, dressing themselves as independently as possible then they will obviously find doing these things in school much easier.'

Dealing with anxiety

It is natural to view your child's first step into the world of formal schooling with some apprehension. Starting school is a big and major milestone in the life of any child and his/her family. Even when the event has been well prepared for and you and your child are looking forward to it, there may still be some concerns and worries. Talking with other parents, your child's school and the class teacher will hopefully help. You might find that the more positive and relaxed you are as parents, then the more at ease your child will be.

When young children begin school, in many ways they are still at the stage of learning how to learn. How they perform in these very early years does not necessarily indicate how they will achieve or succeed later. So there is no point in us putting pressure on our young children to be high achievers.

'Support and encourage your child to go at their own pace.'

All children are different and some learn and progress at a faster rate than others. Some have difficulties in one area of learning or development that others find easy – whether it is social and emotional development or intellectual. Don't compare your child's abilities with the abilities of their siblings, friends or classmates. If you find yourself doing this then remember that children need varying amounts of time to consolidate knowledge and skills before moving on. So support and encourage your child to go at their own pace.

Homeschooling

Some parents, for various reasons, make the decision to homeschool their child right from the start. Some reasons for this may include:

- They believe their children can learn more, or in a better way in a different environment.
- A freer and more flexible curriculum.
- More chance for the child to learn at his/her own pace.
- Less dependency on peers and peer influences.
- Religious and faith reasons.

84

- The child has special or specific needs for which parents feel schools cannot cater well.

- Bad experiences of schools in the past.

If you want to consider homeschooling as an option remember that there are a number of issues to consider first:

- Huge amounts of time, energy and long-term commitment by you to provide your child with a good alternative to mainstream schooling.

- Your child will not benefit from the expertise of qualified teachers and their subject experience.

- Cost. You will need to be able to meet the costs of devoting time to teach, finding tutors and ensuring your child joins and takes part in activities and groups with other children.

- Your child will miss out on the socialisation that happens in classrooms. Children of all social backgrounds, family types, race and faith groups attend most schools. Homeschooling may limit the contact children have to fewer social groups.

If you feel you are able to address the disadvantages and homeschool your child right from preschool age, then you don't need to contact your Local Education Authority to inform them of your choice to do so. If your child's name is already on the entry list for a particular school, then contact the school to tell them your arrangements have changed. If your child has recently started school and you make the decision to home educate, then you will need to contact your Local Education Authority. Some authorities will want proof that you are providing a good and adequate alternative and may home visit. Homeschooling is perfectly legal. At the time of writing this book, the only legal requirement for parents is that their child receives an adequate education during the years of compulsory schooling, but this does not have to be in school.

Useful sources of further information and support for parents who choose home education are:

- Home Education in the UK see www.home-ed.info.

- School House (Scotland wide).

- AHed (covers England, Wales and Northern Ireland).

- HE Special (special educational needs).
- Education Otherwise.
- See the help list at the end of this book for contact details.

Summing Up

- Beginning school is a big step for all children. Hopefully, for most children and their families, it is also an exciting and positive one.

- If your child has attended and enjoyed preschool nurseries or activities with other children and experienced time away from you, the main carer, then the transition from being a preschool to school-age child is likely to go more smoothly.

- Remember that all children are different and, on the whole, will develop and learn at their own pace.

- With their parents' and teachers' support and encouragement, the majority of children soon adjust to and benefit from this new stage in their lives.

- A lot of parents say they feel some sadness when their child begins school. This stage marks the end of the preschool years and, for some parents, the end of longer amounts of time to spend with their child in the way they want to.

- Holidays may have to be restricted to school holiday times, childcare after school and during holidays may need to be rethought and rearranged.

- It is a time of change for the whole family. But also an exciting time! Your child will be making new friends, becoming more independent, developing new interests and benefiting from new opportunities.

- There is a lot to be said for the idea that we 'grow with our children'. We may not always know what is around the corner for them and may wonder how we will deal with new stages in their lives. But all our children are remarkable individuals. It helps to see the changes, and watching them grow and develop as a fascinating privilege.

Help List

Organisations of interest to parents and carers of preschool children.

Arts and crafts

Tel: 0794 282 5114
Email: doodle@doodleandsplat.co.uk
www.doodleandsplat.co.uk
Art and craft classes for under 5s in Dunfermline, Dalgety Bay, Kirkcaldy and Edinburgh.

AHed

Action For Home Education, PO Box 7324, Derby, DE1 OGT
Email form on website
www.ahed.org.uk
Home education information.

Baby massage

International Association of Infant Massage, IAIM UK Chapter, Unit 10, Marlborough Business Centre, 96 George Lane, South Woodford, London, E18 1AD
Tel: (for general enquiries): 020 8989 9597
To email use the contact form on their website.
www.iaim.org.uk
Information about what baby massage is, the benefits and how to find a class.

Baby reflexology

Jenny Lee, High House, High Street, Ewelme, Oxfordshire, OX10 6HQ
Email info@babyreflex.co.uk
Tel:: 01491 839227
www.babyreflex.co.uk
For more information about reflexology for babies and how to find a practitioner near you.

Baby signing

Tiny Talk, Unit 3 The Dairy, Tllehouse Farm Offices, East Shalford Lane, Guildford, GU4 8AE
Tel: 01483 301444
Email: sandrineadmin@tinytalk.co.uk
www.tinytalk.co.uk
Information about baby signing and how to find a class near you.

Box of Ideas

The Dyscovery Centre, University of Wales, Newport, NP20 5DA
Tel: 01633 432330
Email: discoverycentre@newport.ac.uk
www.boxofideas.org
A website written by professionals from The Dyscovery Centre, University of Wales. It gives advice and ideas for parents, teachers and others regarding the issues affecting children from early years to young adulthood. The early years section includes ideas on helping your child with reading, preparing for school, etc. There are also online discussion posts, issues ranging from potty training, bullying to dealing with specific special needs.

Childcare Link

Opportunity Links Trust Court, Vision Park, Histon, Cambridge, CB4 9PW
Email form on the website
www.childcare.co.uk
Provides details about childcare provision in England and general advice about different aspects of childcare including maternity nurses, private tutors etc.

Day Care Trust

Day Care Trust, 2nd Floor, 73-81 Southwark Bridge Road, London, SE1 ONQ
Tel: 0845 872 6260 (020 7940 7510)
Email for childcare enquiries info@daycaretrust.org.uk
www.daycaretrust.org.uk
A national charity that provides information for parents, carers and teaching staff and all those involved in childcare provision.

Directgov

www.directgov.co.uk
The website with information of all UK public services including education, childcare and other areas that concern families and parents with young children. Follow the links to find the area of interest.

Fisher Price

www.fisherprice.com
Click on 'Games and Activities'
Online games and learning activities suitable for young children.

Froebal Educational Institute

Templeton, 118 Priory Lane, London, SW15 5JW
Tel: 020 8878 7546
Email: office@ifei.co.uk
www.froebal.org.uk
Information about the origins and elements of froebalian education.

HE Special

www.he-special.org.uk
Concerned with issues that affect families who home educate children who have special needs.

Home education

www.home-ed.info
Useful site with information about starting and maintaining home education.

I Can

8 Wakley Street, London, EC1V 7QE
Tel: 0845 225 4073 or 020 7843 2552
Email: info@ican.org.uk
www.ican.org.uk
National charity concerned with children's communication skills. Information for parents and professionals concerned about young children's language and communication difficulties.

Little Chestnuts

www.hilaryhawkes.co.uk/littlechestnuts

Online stories, rhymes and games that enhance pre-literacy and communication skills in three to five-year-olds. To share with your child at home or for children in preschool.

Little Tiger Press

www.littletigerpress.com

Publisher of picture books for preschool age children. Website has downloadable games and activities for young children.

Maria Montessori Institute

26 Lyndhurst Gardens, London, NW3 5NW
Tel: 020 7435 3646
Email info@mariamontessori.org
www.mariamontessori.org

Training organisation for Montessori teachers. Website has information about the principles of the Montessori method.

National Association of Family Information Services

www.familyinformationservices.co.uk

See the directory on their website for contact details and information about your local Family Information Service.

National Childminding Association.

Royal Court, 81 Tweedy Road, Bromley, Kent, BR1 1TG
Tel: 0845 880 0044
Email: info@ncma.org.uk
www.ncma.org.uk

The professional organisation for registered childminders. Their website has information useful to parents.

National Day Nurseries Association

National Early Years Enterprise Centre, Longbow Close, Huddersfield, West Yorkshire, HD2 1GQ
01484 407070
Email: info@ndna.org.uk
www.ndna.org.uk
A charity and membership organisation that represents day nurseries in the UK. It promotes the development and education of young children. Has information for parents about finding and choosing a nursery.

Net Mums

www.netmums.com
An online network of parents offering ideas, chat, advice and information on many aspects of parenting and bringing up children.

Ofsted (Office for Standards in Education, Children's Services and Skills)

Picadilly Gate, Store Street, Manchester, M1 2WD
Tel: 0300 123 1231
enquiries@ofsted.gov.uk
www.ofsted.gov.uk
They inspect and regulate services and promote improvement.

Pre-school Learning Alliance

Pre-school Learning Alliance National Centre, The Fitzpatrick Building,
188 York Way, London, N7 9AD
Tel: 020 7697 2500
Email form on website
www.pre-school.org.uk
Membership organisation for preschools throughout the UK. Website has useful information for parents including publications on child development etc, a 'find a nursery' facility as well as issues concerning the childcare workforce and current practice.

Qualifications and Curriculum Development Agency

Tel: 0300 303 3012
www.qcda.gov.uk
Publishes curriculums and the Early Years Foundation Stage.

Rhythmtime

Rhythmtime Internet Department, 76 Beechwood Park Road, Solihull, B91 1ES
Tel: 0121 711 4224
www.rhythmtime.net
Classes for preschool children that use song and music to promote all round development.

Schools Local Education Authorities UK websites

www.schoolswebdirectory.co.uk
Lists web addresses and contact details of each area's Local Education Authority.

School House

Contact email form on the website.
www.schoolhouse.org.uk
An information site for parents and young people who are homeschooling in Scotland.

Sesame Street

www.sesamestreet.org/games
Online games for preschool children that help with language, numeracy, shape recognition as well as games that increase knowledge and awareness of topics such as animals, the seasons, neighbourhood, etc.

Steiner Waldorf Schools Fellowship

11 Church Street, Stourbridge, DY8 1LT
Tel: 01384 374116
Email: admin@steinerwaldorf.org
www.steinerwaldorf.org
Information about the Steiner Waldorf method of education.

Talkingtots

108 Warton Street, Lytham, FY8 5HA
Tel: 01253 735355
Email: form on website
www.talkingtots.info
Interactive classes for preschool children that boost communication and
social skills.

National Association of Toy and Leisure Libraries

1a Harmood Street, London,
NW1 8DN
www.natll.org.uk
Information about toy libraries.

Tumbletots UK Ltd

Blue Bird Park, Bromsgrove, Hunnington, Halesowen, West Midlands, B62 OTT
Tel: 01215 857003
Email: contact form on website
www.tumbletots.com
Preschool sessions which help children develop physical co-ordination, agility
and balance.

Book List

Baby's First Year: A Parent's Guide
By Shanta Everington, Need2Know Books, Peterborough, 2010.

Child Care and Education
By Tina Bruce and Carolyn Meggitt, Hodder and Stoughton, London, 2005

Child Development, An Illustrated Guide
By Carolyn Meggitt and Gerald Sunderland, Heinemann, Oxford, 2001.

Children's Friendships: The Beginnings of Intimacy (Understanding Children's Worlds)
By Judy Dunn, Wiley-Blackwell, Oxford, 2004.

Does my Child Have a Speech Problem?
By Katherine L Martin, Chicago Review Press, Chicago, 1997.

From Birth to Five Years, Children's Developmental Progress
By Mary Sheridan, Routledge, London, 2005.

Getting Ready to Start School
By Hollie Smith and Netmums, Headline, London, 2008.

Learning Without School
By Ross Mountney, Jessica Kingsley Publishers, London, 2008.

Monsters Under the Bed and Other Childhood Fears
By S Garber, R Freedman Spizman, M Daniels Garber, Villard Books, New York, 2003.

Planning Play and the Early Years
By Penny Tassori and Karen Hucker, Heinmann, Oxfrord, 2004

Play in Early Childhood, From Birth to Six Years
By Mary Sheridan, Routledge, London, 2005.

Primary School: A Parent's Guide
By Kim Thomas, Need2Know Books, Peterborough, 2010.

Siblings Without Rivalry
By Adele Faber, Elaine Mazlish and Kimberley Ann Coe, Piccadilly Press Ltd, London, 1999.

Special Educational Needs: A Parent's Guide
By Antonia Chitty and Victoria Dawson, Need2Know Books, Peterborough, 2011.

The Secret of Childhood
By Maria Montessori, Ballantine, New York, 1972.

The Terrible Twos: A Parent's Guide
By Shanta Everington, Need2Know Books, Peterborough, 2010.

Thinking of Home Schooling? First What You Should Know
By Caroline Booker, Kindle eBook, 2011.

Time to Play: In Early Childhood Education
By Tina Bruce, Hodder Arnold, London, 1991.

Toddling to Ten
By Hollie Smith and Netmums, Headline, London, 2008.

Why Love Matters. How Affection Shapes a Baby's Brain
By Sheila Gerhalt, Brunner, Routledge, Sussex and New York, 2004.

Young Children Learning: Talking and Thinking at Home and School,
By Barbara Tizard and Martin Hughes, Fontana Press (Harper Collins), London, 1984.

Glossary

Cognition
Learning, thinking and problem solving processes in the brain.

Dynamic tripod grip
Holding the pencil/pen between the thumb and first two fingers.

Dyslexia
A learning difficulty mainly connected with reading, writing and spelling.

Dyspraxia
A motor or movement co-ordination disability.

Early Years Foundation Stage (EYFS)
A framework that promotes the all-round development of children up to the age of five.

Foundation Stage 3, 2, 1 (FS3, 2, 1)
Refers to the three years before a child reaches primary school Year 1 age. FS3 is roughly preschool or two to three years of age; FS2 is around three to four years of age and FS1 is four to five or Reception class age.

Free-flow play
Children are allowed to move freely from one activity to another, indoors and outdoors without strict time restraints that limit how long they are allowed at each activity or allowed in each area.

Individual Behaviour Plan (IBP)
Similar to an IEP, but with an emphasis on improving and developing the child's behaviour. Methods and goals will be suggested. Used with children who have special needs.

Individual Education Plan (IEP)
A plan made, after assessing and observing a child, that suggests aims and goals that the child can work towards in order to make progress in learning and development. Used with children who have special needs.

Individual Learning Plan (ILP)
A plan made, after assessing and observing a child, that suggests aims and goals that the child can work towards in order to achieve the next stage of learning and development. Used with all children in early years classes/settings.

Kinaesthetic
Refers to a sense of touch and movement.

Moro reflex
An involuntary 'startle' reaction shown by newborn babies.

Neurological
Refers to the way the brain and nervous system works. A neurological disorder is one that is caused by the brain or nervous system working in a way that is not typical.

Object permanence
People and objects still exist even when we cannot see them.

Ofsted
Office for Standards in Education, Children's Services and Skills.

Parentese
Speech used by parents to their babies i.e. 'baby talk'.

Pincer grip
Holding something between the thumb and first two fingers.

Reception class
A school class for four to five-year-olds. May also be called the Foundation Stage 1 class. From this class children progress to Year 1.

SENCO
Special Educational Needs Co-ordinator. The member of staff responsible for the learning and other needs of children with special needs.

Social referencing
In young children, this refers to the way they look to their carers/teachers for 'approval' or 'feedback' before proceeding with an action or behaviour or whilst carrying out the action or behaviour.

Statement of Special Educational Needs
A special report that describes a child's special needs or diagnosis.

Symbolic play

Pretending to be someone else through role play.

Theory of mind

The understanding that others have their own thoughts, views, feelings and emotions separate to our own. The ability to understand other's minds.

Voluntary preschool provision

Preschools that are part of the voluntary sector have a core of paid and trained staff and other staff/helpers who are voluntary. Volunteer parents often make up the preschool's committee. Playgroups that are part of the Pre-school Learning Alliance are examples of voluntary provision.

Need · 2 · Know

Available Titles Include ...

Allergies A Parent's Guide
ISBN 978-1-86144-064-8 £8.99

Autism A Parent's Guide
ISBN 978-1-86144-069-3 £8.99

Blood Pressure The Essential Guide
ISBN 978-1-86144-067-9 £8.99

Dyslexia and Other Learning Difficulties
A Parent's Guide ISBN 978-1-86144-042-6 £8.99

Bullying A Parent's Guide
ISBN 978-1-86144-044-0 £8.99

Epilepsy The Essential Guide
ISBN 978-1-86144-063-1 £8.99

Your First Pregnancy The Essential Guide
ISBN 978-1-86144-066-2 £8.99

Gap Years The Essential Guide
ISBN 978-1-86144-079-2 £8.99

Secondary School A Parent's Guide
ISBN 978-1-86144-093-8 £9.99

Primary School A Parent's Guide
ISBN 978-1-86144-088-4 £9.99

Applying to University The Essential Guide
ISBN 978-1-86144-052-5 £8.99

ADHD The Essential Guide
ISBN 978-1-86144-060-0 £8.99

Student Cookbook – Healthy Eating The Essential Guide
ISBN 978-1-86144-069-3 £8.99

Multiple Sclerosis The Essential Guide
ISBN 978-1-86144-086-0 £8.99

Coeliac Disease The Essential Guide
ISBN 978-1-86144-087-7 £9.99

Special Educational Needs A Parent's Guide
ISBN 978-1-86144-116-4 £9.99

The Pill An Essential Guide
ISBN 978-1-86144-058-7 £8.99

University A Survival Guide
ISBN 978-1-86144-072-3 £8.99

View the full range at **www.need2knowbooks.co.uk**.
To order our titles call **01733 898103**, email **sales@ n2kbooks.com** or visit the website. Selected ebooks available online.

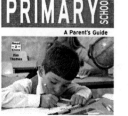
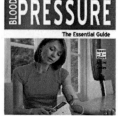

Need - 2 - Know, Remus House, Coltsfoot Drive, Peterborough, PE2 9BF